Astrological Lore
of All Ages

ASTROLOGICAL LORE OF ALL AGES

Elbert Benjamine

The Church of Light
Los Angeles

Your purchase of this Church of Light book helps bring an expanded view of Universal Welfare to a world in search of new spiritual meaning. Royalties are used by a non-profit organization whose mission is to teach, practice and disseminate The Religion of the Stars.

Astrological Lore of All Ages may be obtained through your local bookstore, or you may order it from The Church of Light, 2341 Coral Street, Los Angeles, CA 90031-2916, (213)226-0453.

Portions of this book not exceeding a total of 2,000 words may be freely quoted or reprinted without permission provided credit is given in the following form:

Reprinted from *Astrological Lore of All Ages* by Elbert Benjamine. ©1993 by The Church of Light.

1st Printing - 1945, Aries Press, Chicago
2nd Printing - 1993, Church of Light, Los Angeles

Library of Congress Cataloging-in-Publication Data
Benjamine, Elbert.
    Common traditions among the stellar religion of ancient Egypt, Chaldea, and the North and Central Americas; Astrological significance of Holidays. / Elbert Benjamine.
— 2nd printing, 1st ed.
    Astrological lore of all ages / Elbert Benjamine
        p.   cm.
    ISBN 0-87887-366-X
    Orginally published: Chicago : Aries Press. 1945.
    1. Astrology—History. I. Title
BF1671.B46   1993   93-10698
133.5 ' 09—dc20   CIP

The Church of Light
2341 Coral Street
Los Angeles, CA 90031-2916

Contents

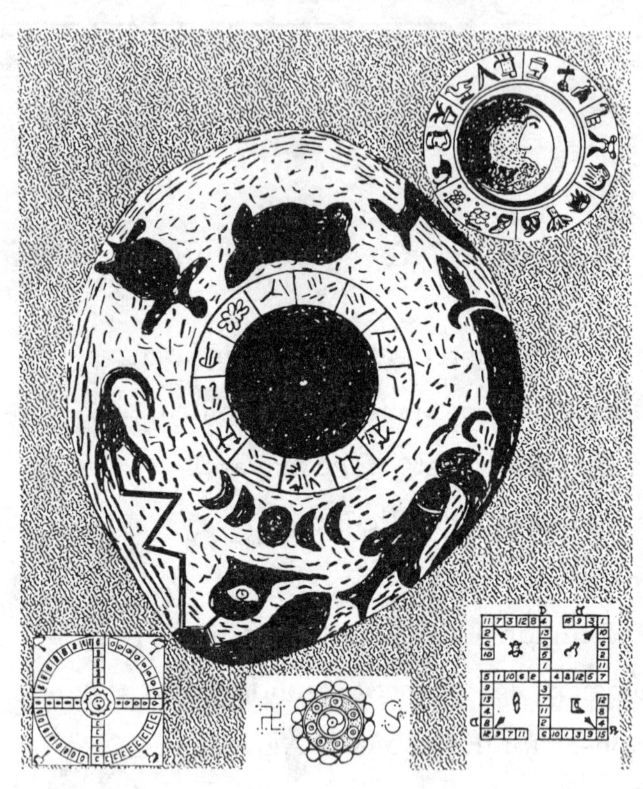

Chapter 1

Stellar Religion and Healing of Akhenaten

hrough the efforts of Arthur Weigall, who served brilliantly for so many years as Inspector General of Antiquities in Egypt, historians are now able to reconstruct in detail the circumstances surrounding the life of Egypt's most spiritual ruler, Akhenaten. Mr. Weigall's last works, published just before he died—from the curses placed by the Priests of the Shadow to protect the tomb of the one who had restored them to power—through a careful comparison of all discoveries, have for the first time given a complete series of precise dates and events in Egypt's past.

As Lord Carnarvon was the first, so Mr. Weigall was the twentieth among those closely associated with the opening of the tomb of King Tutankhamen to meet an unusual and untimely death. When the tomb was opened in 1923 Weigall was in vigorous health. He immediately fell ill, and after suffering from a lingering and mysterious malady, passed to the next plane early in 1934 at the age of fifty-three.

The list of events with precise datings which Mr. Weigall worked out lend value to many interesting occurrences which heretofore have rested solely upon tradition. And by uniting tradition to what is now historical record, we are able to get a clear picture of the struggle by which, at one period, spiritual ideas of the most exalted order gained national acceptance.

Since the sinking of Atlantis and Mu there have at all times been those on earth who were familiar with the ancient spiritual wisdom. But the only time when the light shone full strength in Egypt and The Religion of the Stars was adopted by the nation as a whole was during the reign and due to the efforts of our brother, Akhenaten. As the world has now entered a cycle, or astral stream, of similar quality but of far greater power, drastic events are transpiring which—due allowance being made for environmental circumstances—are somewhat parallel to those which happened in his day. We may therefore scan that past with considerable profit. And while tradition should not be neglected, yet in the interest of clear analysis it should ever be thus labeled, and not confused with recorded fact. Consequently, in what follows that which is tradition will be thus designated, and that which is of historical record, and all quotations used, will be drawn from the works of Arthur Weigall.

History records that at the time of the early Sumerian kings in Chaldea the first dynasty of Lower Egypt was established, dated according to the Turin MS., 5507 B.C. At this time no suitable calendar was in use and the Egyptian system of writing had not been evolved. Fifty kings were to reign before Menes, who is commonly considered the first historical ruler because seven years after he came to the throne he established a calendar by which succeeding events could be, and were, recorded.

Menes, who thus established the First Dynasty, came to the throne 3407 B.C. A dynasty usually consisted of a series of rulers who were close blood kin. When the country was conquered by an invader, or some event such as a revolution permitted a new family to take charge, this commonly established a new dynasty. In the First Dynasty there were 8 kings, in the Second Dynasty 9 kings, in the Third Dynasty 6 kings.

The Third Dynasty is interesting to us because the second king, Tosortho, 2868–2850 B.C., was revered as a philosopher, proverb maker, physician, scribe and architect. At Sakkara he built what is known as the Step Pyramid, a rough square 351 by 393 feet, of six monstrous steps totaling nearly 200 feet in height, the largest stone edifice up to that time. Then came the sixth king of the Third Dynasty, Snofru, 2813–2790 B.C., who built a stone pyramid just southwest of Memphis which, still 326 feet high and 700 feet at base, is almost as large as the Great Pyramid. Many traditions exist as to the influence of initiates in the life of Snofru. He also built a second pyramid. And immediately following him there commenced the Fourth Dynasty, although there seems to be no adequate political or hereditary reason why Khufu, who succeeded him, should be considered of a different dynasty.

Khufu, whom the Greeks called Cheops, was thus the first king of the Fourth Dynasty. He ruled 2789–2767 B.C., the dynasty as a whole, comprising seven kings, 2789–2716 B.C., being probably contemporaneous with the founding of the empire of Sargon the Great in Chaldea. Khufu, or Cheops, employed 100,000 men, during the three months of the year that the population otherwise would have been idle, due to their farms being flooded by the Nile. It took him three years to build the road over which to haul the stone, and twenty more years to build the Great Pyramid. The stones were ferried across the river during high water. The pyramid, which is still one of the greatest wonders of the world, was originally 481 feet high, with a base of 451 feet, and covers 13 acres.

Now for a moment let us turn from recorded history to tradition: Tradition has it that when the darkness settled over Atlantis and Mu, colonists were sent to what later became the seven centers of ancient civilization, and took with them records having to do with the ancient stellar religion. In Egypt there was quarried out, near the town of Ynu, a secret vault in the rock, closed by an immense movable block of sandstone. The knowledge of this Chamber of the Rolls and the Library of Tahuti, which embraced records from Atlantis, was reserved to initiates. Such initiates then, even as today, were ever alert to place true spiritual knowledge before as wide a number of people as possible. But even as today, what thus could be placed before them depended upon the willingness and ability of the people to accept such exalted doctrines.

Even in Atlantis and Mu there was a continuous struggle upon the part of graft, greed, corruption and the inversive side of Pluto to suppress true wisdom and to pervert the spiritual, to the end that what we call priestly and political racketeers might dominate and exploit the people in every possible way. And before their destruction the light had vanished from these two ancient lands.

Of Egypt's seven thousand years of history, with the single exception of a decade under the reign of Akhenaten, the general public had no more knowledge of the true meaning of spirituality, of the real nature of existence after death, of the wider significance and purpose of life, than do the people of the world today. Then, as now, and as at all times, there were some individuals who had received the light, and even among the general public some who had a clearer conception of the spiritual side of things than others. But then, as now, there was the constant effort to keep the people in ignorance and servility.

The rulers of Egypt always were approached by the initiates and given such knowledge of the wisdom religion as they were willing to receive. Some of them, such as Tosortho, Snofru and Khufu went far along the path of true initiation. But so powerful had the priestly group become that, with the exception of Akhenaten, they felt that opposition to them in religious matters would mean a revolution and loss of the throne. Even as in the past powerful financial groups have been the real rulers of the U.S. and many other countries, so in Egypt, in so far as religion and its material spoils system were concerned, the priestly group, with their vast holdings of property, and ability to sway the multitude through superstition, were too powerful to unseat. Yet Tosortho and Snofru availed themselves of the knowledge of initiates who had access to the Library of Tahuti.

Khufu, or Cheops, when he came to the throne, being a very ambitious man, had a great desire to do something which would glorify his name above that of any past or future ruler of Egypt. And following the example of preceding rulers, he decided to build a pyramidal monument for himself. But he wished this pyramid to excel any that later might be constructed. So he sent for an initiate named Didi, who was famed for his learning, and asked his help.

It had been customary for the initiates of Atlantis and Mu, not in the form of a pyramid, but in their various temples, to incorporate measurements and relations which they found to exist as correspondences throughout Nature. That is, in the very masonry of their edifices they had incorporated The Religion of the Stars. And these measurements and correspondences, as well as other wisdom, were on the rolls in the Library of Tahuti. The initiate Didi, employed by Khufu, therefore presented plans for the pyramid which should in its structure embrace the relations between the various phases of Nature, the measurements and as many other correspondences as possible, as recorded in the Library of Tahuti, so that the Great Pyramid of Gizeh should express in stone The Religion of the Stars.

Because the Great Pyramid—which is the only pyramid to contain such measurements and correspondences—is an accurate portrayal of stellar cycles and influences, both past and future, like the Bible it has come to be used as a basis of prophecy. When the premise is correct, that is, when based upon accurate and reliable knowledge of astrological influences, either the Great Pyramid or the Bible can be used to calculate the nature and date of future events. But because of the many who have written books on the subject few have had the required detailed knowledge of astrology to take a proper starting point, or accurately to trace stellar correspondences, almost every variety of drivel possible has been written in relation to Bible prophecy and Pyramid prophecy.

That we are at the end of one dispensation and the commencement of another (the Plutonian Period of the Aquarian Age) the stars point out clearly. But that all the horrible things prophesied are going to come to pass, even though the whole world is undergoing upheaval and radical change, is not foretold in Bible or Pyramid, but is the result of hysteria and a fear complex in the minds of those who, feeling the impact of the new astral energy stream, place upon the inevitable transition of adaptation to the new period and the vast and sanguine struggle involved in making the adaptation, an interpretation which is but the expression of their own inward anxiety.

The Brotherhood of Light—The Church of Light—has set itself the task of making it impossible for any person in the world to be ignorant of the fundamental doctrines of The Religion of the Stars. Let us see whether its traditions coincide with the historical findings of Weigall. In the Declaration of Principles of The Brotherhood of Light (now incorporated as The Church of Light) published in May, 1915, nearly a score of years before Weigall made his study of ancient dates, occurs this passage: "According to our traditions, in the year 2440 B.C. a group separated from the Theocracy of Egypt, and throughout all subsequent times, as a secret order, the name of which translated into English means, The Brotherhood of Light, has been perpetuated."

History records the building of other pyramids than those mentioned, that the Fifth Dynasty, 2715–2588 B.C., embraced 9 kings and that the Sixth Dynasty, 2587–2459 B.C., embraced 6 kings. The last of this line of kings was Menthesuph, who reigned only one year; after which a period of anarchy ensued lasting 6 years. After 6 years of anarchy, which we may well believe was fomented by priestly racketeers striving to dominate the land, Neterkere, the founder of the Seventh Dynasty, came to the throne. But in the year 2452 B.C. he was murdered by the exploiting group, and his sister Nitokris, given his place. After reigning 12 years Nitokris committed suicide.

Weigall quotes Heroditus in regard to the suicide of Nitokris, which preceded the separation of The Brotherhood of Light from a Theocracy which had become irreparably corrupt and bent on keeping the people in superstition, that they might profit thereby. It seems that the nobles who comprised the political group—which we may be sure were incited by the Priests of the Shadow, as these constantly strove to dominate the policies of the throne—having murdered her brother and placed her on the throne, commenced to exert undue pressure upon Queen Nitokris. Perhaps she had the enlightenment of the people at heart. At all events, she arrived at a point where she realized she could no longer resist the demands of this iniquitous group. She therefore had a building erected near the river on a low-lying site which was well below the level of the Nile floods, and she had a fine hall built as a cellar beneath it, such as those now to be seen in the temple of Denderah, but larger. Secretly she had a tunnel made which should bring the flood water directly to the building. Then she gave a royal banquet to which she invited all these treacherous nobles. As soon as they were in the crypt enjoying themselves, she went above, closed the trap door, turned on the water, and drowned the lot. Having accomplished this, and knowing, we may believe, the power of the priestly racketeers who had used the nobles for their own ends, she committed suicide by shutting herself in a room filled with charcoal fumes.

No wonder The Brotherhood of Light, in order to persist, became a secret organization. The priests of Amen grew to be the strongest group in Egypt. They had vast holdings, levied immense financial tribute, and had built at Karnak and Luxor stupendous temples. With the characteristic cunning of the Lower-Pluto forces, they taught the nobles that to give their daughters to be Brides of Amen was an honor. These Brides of Amen, recruited from among the most attractive maidens of the land, were dedicated to temple service. That is, they were prostitutes who catered to the services of those who had money; but the money they received for their prostitution was made holy by giving it to the priests. When they grew too old to be attractive, and thus failed to yield a good revenue to the temple, the priests arranged for them marriage with rich merchants. The merchants were given to understand that this prostitution, because it was to benefit the god Amen, was rather an asset than a detriment to their brides. Such doctrines are everywhere characteristic of the inversive side of Pluto, and we find similar institutions in India today. This is but one of a hundred subtle ways by which an inversive priesthood compel people to do their bidding.

To conserve space, let us now skip the intervening dynasties down to the Eighteenth, which was founded by Ahmouse I in 1580 B.C., over 1,300 years after the building of the great pyramids, and some 2,000 years after Menes founded the first recorded dynasty. At this time Amen was the presiding god at Thebes, which had become the capital. Then as rulers came Amenhotep I, followed by Thutmosis I, Thutmosis II, Queen Hatshepsut, Thutmosis III, and Thutmosis IV, who was the grandfather of Akhenaten. Thutmosis IV ascended the throne in 1420 B.C., and Akhenaten's other grandfather, Yuaa, who was not a priest of Amen but of Min, and who was an initiate, was born about 1470 B.C.

Probably due to this initiate, Yuaa, even before Akhenaten came to the throne, the wife of Amenhotep III, Queen Tiy, mother of Akhenaten and daughter of Yuaa, had endeavored to suppress the power and iniquities of the dark priests of Amen. The organization of Amen had its headquarters at Karnak. Led by the hand of Tiy, who was called the Great Queen, Amenhotep III came to be known as the Magnificent. When Amenhotep III died, in the 36th year of his reign, Queen Tiy assumed control on behalf of her 13 year old boy, Amenhotep IV. And subsequent events indicate that he was given opportunity to gain the wisdom of his grandfather, Yuaa, the initiate. Amenhotep IV who thus ascended the throne in 1375 B.C. through the death of his father, was born 1388 B.C. He early realized how completely his people were dominated by the shadow of the Lower-Pluto priests, and he determined to free them from such inversive influences. At that time Amenism, with its magical rites, its many gods, its complicated rituals, and its host of corrupt priests, was the official religion of Egypt. As Ra, the sun-god, was universally venerated by the public, these cunning priests of Amen, ever alert to political advantage, joined the name of Ra to Amen, so that the chief deity of the time was often referred to as Amen-Ra.

The king, surrounded by these priests, remained in the orthodox faith of Amen, as signified by the name he inherited, Amenhotep, until he was nineteen years of age. At that time he contacted the same spiritual source from which now emanates The Brotherhood of Light lessons. [*ed. see list of courses on page 00*] This led him to perceive that the orthodox religion of Amen kept the minds of the people confused as to reality, steeped in fear, servile to the priests, and shut from them the knowledge which would lead to true spirituality, progress and happiness.

Ra, as worshiped in his time, was the disc of the sun. But behind that disc Amenhotep IV perceived an all-pervading spiritual intelligence, of which the physical sun is only the symbol. And it became his ambition to establish a nonmaterialistic religion of Life, Light and Love, free from the graven images, incantations, and curses which encumbered Amenism. When the king became one of the Brethren of the Light, he determined to spread the gospel of The Religion of the Stars, even as The Church of Light has determined to spread it to the world of today. But having allied himself with the Legions of Light, he could no longer bear the name of Amen, a name denoting orthodoxy and its spiritual darkness.

Already at 16 or 17 years of age, in spite of the priests, he had introduced Stellar Art. At 19 the king decided the time was ripe to make his convictions clear to all. He therefore renounced the name Amenhotep, with its implication of obedience to Amen. And, in choosing a name to take the place of the one discarded, he joined the words which expressed his religion of Life, Light and Love. Aten means light. To indicate to his subjects that he was a Brother of the Light, he called himself Akhenaten, meaning Living in the Light. Having changed his name, he commenced a vigorous campaign to establish the religion of Atenism (Light), and to eradicate the worship of the numerous gods and elementals of Amenism. He taught his people there was a single, supreme, all-pervading, spiritual Deity, symbolized by Aten, or Light.

The vast material resources of Amen, with huge temples at Karnak, and their dominion at Thebes, with their spies at every hand, soon convinced the young king that he could not combat the Lower-Pluto forces amid surroundings so permeated with their accomplices and magic. He decided, therefore, to move the capital and to collect about him in it only those who were willing to live constructively, willing to learn the truths of Nature, and who were willing to defy the power of the Amen priesthood.

Akhenaten was only 19 when, having made this decision, he sailed down the river from Thebes to a point which was suitable for his purpose, some 160 miles above modern Cairo, and there founded the City of the Horizon. After two years of feverish work a city there had arisen which, for beauty and art, perhaps has had no parallel in history. Here at the age of 21 he took up his residence amid the many who, perceiving his wisdom and spiritual greatness, had joined forces with him. From this new city, which was magnetized to his own spiritual ideas, he was successful, for the first time in recorded history, in suppressing corruption, dissipating ignorance, and spreading The Religion of the Stars throughout the length and breadth of the land.

To set forth all he taught would be to present the 21 Brotherhood of Light courses; for these, in modern terminology and with reference to the findings of modern science, are merely a present-day interpretation of the same teachings which Akhenaten derived from his study of the rolls in the Library of Tahuti. He taught the constructive use of astrological knowledge. Instead of the curses and maledictions of Amen, he taught the use of beauty, of art, and of all enobling activities to lead the mind into channels which are completely constructive.

While Akhenaten occupied the throne greed, corruption and exploitation were suppressed, and fear, hatred and vengeance were removed from religion. According to Weigall he taught that God: "Was the tender, loving Father of all men, ever-present and ever-mindful of his creatures. There dropped not a sigh from the lips of a babe that the intangible Aten did not hear; no lamb bleated for its mother but the remote Aten hastened to soothe it. He was the loving Father and Mother of all that he had made, who brought up millions by His bounty."

"As Akhenaten had completely revolutionized the beliefs of Egypt as to the nature of God, so he altered and purged the theories regarding the existence of the soul after death. According to the old beliefs, the soul of man had to pass through awful places up to the judgment throne of Osiris, where he was weighed in the balances. If he was found wanting he was devoured by a ferocious monster, but if the scales turned in his favor he was accepted into the Elysian fields. So many were the spirits, bogies, and demigods which he was likely to meet before the goal was reached that he had to know by heart a tedious string of formulae, the correct repetition of which, and the correct making of the related magic, alone ensured his safe passage. Akhenaten flung all these formulae into the fire, even Osiris himself with all his court."

The doctrine of hell and eternal punishment, the fear which so often warps and cripples the child's little mind and drives afar the possibility of a happy adult life, were no part of his teachings. Instead, due allowance being made for the difference in times and other circumstances, his teachings relative to the next life were practically identical with those set forth in Brotherhood of Light Course XX, *The Next Life.*

With so many powerful enemies it is not to be wondered that Akhenaten died in his thirtieth year. He had arrayed himself as the opponent of all the selfish, brutal, inversive, ruthless and cruel Lower-Pluto forces. Yet during the ten or eleven years just preceding his death he had the satisfaction of building up a superior culture, and of observing his people devoted to the religion of light, which is The Religion of the Stars.

He left no son to succeed him, and Smenkhhkara, husband of his eldest daughter, ruled but a few months. He was not sufficiently obedient to the priests who carried out the will of the Lower-Pluto forces. Then the husband of the third daughter came to the throne. The Lower-Pluto forces were pleased with him. This son-in-law of Akhenaten, who delivered the populace back into the power of the Lower-Pluto priests, was none other than Tutankhamen (note the ending), whose unspoiled tomb was opened in 1923 amid worldwide notoriety. He immediately restored the priests of Amen, with the result that polytheism soon flourished again.

Akhenaten, as a Brother of Light, had no use for curses, no use for war, no use for fear, no use for vengeance. But the priests of Amen were Brethren of the Shadows. And there can be no doubt that the sudden tragedies which dogged the footsteps of all those who were present at the opening of Tutankhamen's tomb were due to the curses placed to guard it by the priests of Amen. Lord Carnarvon and his party within a few years, one by one, felt the weight of the curses placed by the Lower-Pluto priests to protect the tomb of the one who had restored them to power.

Many writings of Akhenaten have been studied by scholars, and historians record: "Such a synthesis of life and religion is unique in the world's history. Life was rich and beautiful, joyous and free, not in spite of, but because of religion. For the religion was one from which the master mind of Akhenaten had banished superstition and fear and into which he had introduced sunshine and happiness." Reading this one cannot but think of the inhibitions of Puritanism, and the doctrine of hell and eternal punishment, believed in by some even at present.

As to the man himself, Arthur Weigall says: "He has given us an example three thousand years ago which might be followed at the present day; an example of what a husband and father should be, of what an honest man should do, of what a poet should feel, of what a preacher should teach, of what an artist should strive for, of what a scientist should believe, of what a philosopher should think."

Among other things he created a new art, Stellar Art, and developed a method of treatment, Stellar Healing. All the essentials of this Stellar Healing are set forth in sufficient detail in the language of symbolical pictograph in his Stellar Art, so that were no other source of information available to us on this subject it would be possible to learn it all from the many pictures he has left.

Quoting from the *Story of Religion,* by Charles Francis Potter:

> With true artistic taste Akhenaten devised a symbol to illustrate what he meant. There began to appear before long, on the walls of the temple and tombs, pictures of various scenes in the life of the king, pictures which have lasted even until today.
>
> Above each scene is portrayed the disc of the sun with distinct rays descending to certain parts of the bodies of the human beings in the picture and to the more prominent objects. Each ray terminated in a miniature hand and some of the hands holding the ankh, the ancient Egyptian symbol of life.

Without consuming many printed pages with descriptions of the pictures of this kind left by Akhenaten, their purport insofar as Stellar Healing is concerned can be summed up in four general ideas as follows, more details of which will be discussed later:

1. Planetary energies reaching man not only map his character

at birth, but exert definite influences over him, at times which can be predetermined, throughout the whole of his life. This is pictured by the rays descending to certain parts of the bodies of human beings.

2. The physical environment by which he is surrounded, each item of which also is influenced by planetary energies, also exerts an influence upon man. To what extent this physical influence opposes or cooperates with the planetary energies operative at a given time must be ascertained by observation of the physical environment. This is pictured by the various objects by which the human beings in the picture are surrounded.

3. The events and conditions which are present at any given time in an individual's life are the offspring of his character as it exists at that time, energized by such planetary energies as then reach it, and acting upon the available physical environment, which influences both the trend and the importance of what occurs. This is pictured by both rays and objects adjacent to human beings.

4. The amount of control which an individual can exercise over what takes place in his life at a given time depends upon two factors whose relative importance constantly varies, but which on the average are of about equal power: Upon his ability to energize and modify in the desired direction the factors of his character which respond to planetary energy; and upon his ability to select physical environmental conditions which offer little resistance to the events he desires.

Stellar Diagnosis

One thought explained by the rays which represent the energies of a planet descending to the part of the body mapped by a planet in the chart of birth or to objects in the environment ruled by that planet, is that all the planets derive the energies which they transmit to life on the earth from the sun. It is the same conception set forth in B. of L. lesson No. 41, page 78, thus:

> The planets revolving about the sun in elliptical paths cut the energy field of the sun. This is not an electromagnetic field only, but also an astral energy field and a spiritual energy field. And the planets cutting this huge energy field in turn become transformers and transmitters of energy. That is, each being of different chemical

composition and different density of material, they each are adapted to picking up energies and stepping them down to certain frequencies and radiating these into space.

That these energies radiated by the planets have a profound influence upon things of the earth is shown by the rays extending to those things on earth. Those extending to portions of the human anatomy indicate that the planetary energies chiefly affect those portions of the human body mapped by a given planet in the birthchart. That is, if Mars is in Sagittarius in the birthchart, the energy from Mars is chiefly received in the thighs. Thus did Akhenaten, in his art, set forth the doctrine that any condition of life could be diagnosed by astrological means. Over and over in art, some of which persists to the present day, he emphasized the paramount importance of Stellar Diagnosis.

While diseases of the physical body—as explained in detail in the book, *Body Disease and Its Stellar Treatment*—were thus diagnosed, these were not set completely apart from other conditions in human life. Every event and condition which came into the individual's life, whether affecting his health, his purse, his domestic relations, his honor, or his morality, had Birthchart Constants which revealed his predisposition toward it, and Progressed Constants which indicated when these predispositions, under the influence of planetary energy, would be more apt to develop into the event or condition the probability or possibility of which was thus astrologically foreshown. An extensive and rapidly growing list of such Birthchart Constants and Progressed Constants is given in the three books, *How To Select A Vocation*, *When and What Events Will Happen* and *Body Disease and Its Stellar Treatment*.

Stellar Healing

Diagnosis, however, as Akhenaten well realized, no matter through what means correctly made, of itself gives no help to humanity. Diagnosis merely indicates what condition exists and why it is present. For the individual to benefit in any manner from diagnosis, he must know what to do to change the condition and then do the thing which will make the indicated change. There is no better recognized symbol of doing something than the human hand. And to indicate that through doing specific things mankind could, and should, exercise control over its life, and overcome its afflictions, Akhenaten placed miniature human hands at the ends of the various planetary rays. These hands referred to a specific method of treatment of disease, and also in a larger sense to whatever activities enabled the individual to acquire a more complete control over his own life.

The sun, from which the planetary rays were pictured as extending to the earth, not only portrayed the source of the energy which the planets transmitted, but was also the symbol of the whole inner plane environment. Light which comes from the sun is immaterial. Only that which has rest mass can be considered material, and photons, which are the bundles of energy of which light is composed, have no rest mass. Yet even the most unobservant cannot have failed to notice, from the difference in the behavior of vegetation in the presence and absence of light, that this immaterial energy has a profound influence over life on the earth.

Aten, or light, to Akhenaten and his followers, not only represented the intelligence of the supreme, all-pervading Deity, but also the whole inner plane environment. Intuitively he grasped 3300 years ago what we have only of late years come to recognize, that the inner plane and any of its forces can only contact the physical plane through energies which have approximately the velocity of light. Light now is classified as one small band in the electromagnetic spectrum, which at one end embraces the Hertzian waves which are from 5,000 miles to $\frac{1}{32}$ inch long, through infra red waves, visible light, ultra violet waves, up through X-rays to the gamma waves at the other end. There are about 60,000 waves of visible light to the inch, about 100,000 gamma rays in the length of one wave of visible light; but all these electromagnetic waves have one thing in common: they all have in free space the same velocity as light. Thus even as the velocity of light is taken as the one thing which remains constant in modern physics, and as energies having this velocity are the only means of communicating between inner plane and outer plane, so did Akhenaten use light to indicate the influence of inner plane forces and the all-pervading intelligence of the Supreme Being, which could be contacted only through moving the consciousness to higher levels of the inner plane.

He devised methods by which, as explained in Brotherhood

of Light Course XVI, *Stellar Healing*, the electromagnetic energies of the healer could be used to gather up and transmit to the patient such planetary energies as were necessary temporarily to change the character, or thought structure, of the patient. And he developed the science of Mental Alchemy by which, as explained for specific difficulties in the books, *Stellar Dietetics, When and What Events Will Happen,* and *Body Disease and Its Stellar Treatment,* the healer or the patient himself could effectively use the power of thought to change the character, or thought structure, in such a manner as to enable it the better to overcome afflictions or gain such results as were desired in any selected department of life.

The Role of Physical Environment
But he did not overlook the fact that whenever any physical change is to be brought about, the physical condition thus to be changed offers a certain resistance. That resistance to change, such as any event or alteration in the condition of life implies, varies— as is illustrated by diagrams in the book, *Progressed Aspects of Standard Astrology*—according to factors which are not shown in the birthchart and progressed aspects of the individual. But however small or large that resistance may be, the energies of his character, or thought cell structure, must be of sufficient intensity and volume to overcome that resistance before physical changes affecting his life take place.

Other objects and other people are affected by planetary energies. But the manner in which they are affected is not completely shown in the chart of the person who is influenced by these other objects and people. Not only do the planetary energies affect his thought structure, but his contacts with objects and other people also affect it. Yet neither the special trends given the thought cell activity by these factors of the external environment nor the influence exerted at a particular time by the physical environment can be completely ascertained from the birthchart and progressed aspects of the individual affected. They can only be adequately ascertained by a competent analysis of the physical environment both past and present.

Thus both in diagnosis and in healing, Akhenaten gave about equal weight to the influence of the planets and the influence of physical environment. He did not feel that a condition of the physical body, for instance, coincident with lack of proper foods could be corrected merely by proper thinking. Nor did he believe that proper foods, without a change in thinking, would bring health. Nor in any other department of life did he believe that attention should be given only to the factors of one plane; but that the power of inner plane energies, such as those of thoughts and the planets, and the resistances of the physical plane, such as those exercised by people and objects, both should be given about equal consideration. His healing, which embraced improving any condition in the life as desired, called for intelligent action to be taken to change both the trend of expression of the thought structure, or soul, and equally intelligent action to be taken to secure the proper physical environment to facilitate the work of the soul in bringing the desired condition or event into the life.

The Interaction of the Soul With Both Planes
I will try to give his conception of the manner in which events and conditions are brought into an individual's life in my own words, and in terms of the factors which extensive Case History Studies Of Environment And Conditioning As Affecting Events Attracted By Progressed Aspects indicate to be effective.

An individual is born. Within not too rigid limits the positions of the signs and planets in the birthchart map, due consideration being paid to his evolutionary level, the activity and harmony or discord of each of the ten thought cell families and with which departments of life they are chiefly associated. The general trends of the character at birth can only express through the physical conditions by which the youngster finds himself surrounded. The Mars energies will express in a Mars way, and the Saturn energies will express in a Saturn way, and they will express through the departments of life mapped by the houses ruled by the planet in the chart of birth; but the specific channels through which they are thus permitted to express Conditions them to express more readily through similar channels again. Thus the outlet which has already been found for the expression of a harmony or a discord has a determining influence upon how a similar harmony or a similar discord will again try to express when at any time it is given accessory energy in the future.

Yet no matter how strongly certain thought cells have been Conditioned to express through a specific type of physical event, and no matter how much accessory energy they receive from progressed aspects, they cannot express as that specific event if the physical environment does not afford opportunity for it. If the physical environment offers too much resistance to the specific event toward which there has been consistent conditioning in the past, the energy, seeking the line of least resistance, will express through some other specific event characteristic of the planets involved in the progressed aspect and the houses in the birthchart they rule.

When a progressed aspect is present, the thought cells within the soul receive additional energy as indicated by it. This gives them, in proportion to the power of the progressed aspect, greater activity than they normally possess. It is inevitable that thought cell activity of the kind indicated by the planets involved be stimulated by a progressed aspect. But there is nothing inevitable about what will transpire as the result of this energy added to given thought cells. That depends upon the character as mapped by the birthchart, the conditioning its thought cells have had since birth, the resistance or assistance given a specific expression through thoughts deliberately directed according to mental alchemy, the type of energy the thought cells receive from other progressed aspects acting as Rallying Forces, and the resistance offered by environment to certain events and the facility afforded by it to other events.

A progressed aspect of considerable power may pass by with no other event than a different trend in the thinking, or a different trend to the emotions, accompanied by adequate glandular response. If the conditioning and physical environment offer sufficient resistance to any event characteristic of the planets involved in a progressed aspect, the progressed aspect may come and go, and only affect the thought processes or the emotions. For it is only when the physical environment is weak enough in comparison to the pressure exerted on it by the thought cells of the soul—a pressure which scientists now term the Psychokinetic Effect—operating from the inner plane, that it yields to them and a physical event occurs. The importance of the physical event depends not upon the power of the progressed aspect, but upon the relative strength of the thought cell activity it stimulates and the relative weakness of the physical environment to resist that activity.

An event which is primarily attracted due to the activity of a certain group of thought cells bears the characteristic marks of the planetary energy which is responsible for the thought cell stimulation. But if there are several progressed aspects operative during a given period, and the resistance of physical environment to the expression of one type of event is great, while the resistance to another type indicated by another progressed aspect which is present is small, the total energy of several progressed aspects may express chiefly through an event which is characteristic of the one planet to whose influence the resistance is small.

The specific event which is attracted by a given progressed aspect is not determined by the birthchart and progressed aspects alone. The event will bear the characteristics of the planet chiefly responsible for it, and it will affect one of the departments of life mapped in the birthchart by a house ruled by one of the planets making the progressed aspect. But which one of these houses, and which specific event of several that may affect the department of life ruled by any one of these houses, is determined very largely, not by the progressed aspect, but by the way the individual has been Conditioned previously and by the facilities offered by the physical environment for the thought cell activity to express through one specific event in the category rather than through another.

When both harmonious progressed aspects and discordant progressed aspects are operative at the same time, they may express through different events which are characteristic of each. But if the conditioning and the consequent thinking favor one event which is either harmonious or discordant, and the physical environment also favors the same event, the chief event of the period may bear only the characteristic of the harmony, or the discord, as the case may be. That is, the chief event when both harmonious and discordant progressed aspects are present, may be either harmonious or discordant, depending upon conditioning and physical environment.

The precise timings of the events—see diagram 6 in the book, *Progressed Aspects of Standard Astrology*—which are attracted coincident with progressed aspects are also affected by variations in the resistance offered by physical environment during the period they are operative.

According to the conceptions of Akhenaten, which have now been verified by a vast amount of statistical analysis by The

Brotherhood of Light Astrological Research Department, the specific event which takes place, whether an individual can succeed in a given undertaking, how important the event is, and how fortunate or unfortunate, are all determined not by the birthchart and progressed aspects alone, but by these in relation to previous Conditioning by physical environment and in relation to the resistance at the time offered by physical environment to events of a specific nature, importance, and harmony or discord.

In his healing, consequently, he worked to modify both the activity and the desires of the thought cells, and the resistance of physical environment to the conditions he desired to bring about; devoting his energies thus to alterations in physical environment as well as to alterations within the soul. He taught that Stellar Healing was equally applicable to any undesirable condition in the life, and that the essentials of such healing were always the same: an alteration of the thought structure or the energy possessed by certain thought cells within it, combined with an alteration of the physical environment which would facilitate the work the modified thought cells must do to attract the desired event or condition.

He taught that man should control his life and destiny to the end of Contributing His Utmost to Universal Welfare, and that the degree of success he attains in this depends upon the degree to which he energizes and modifies in the desired direction the thought cells within his soul, and the degree to which he is able to select physical environmental conditions which will afford facility for these modified thought cells to bring to pass the conditions and events he desires.

Posidonius and
the Star Lore of Chaldea

nce more the tides of heaven, reaching their spiritual flood, in turning, leave the shores of our planet strewn with the wreckage of selfish acquisition. And amid this debris may be found the germinating seeds of spiritual endeavor. These seeds of true comprehension have not just been brought in on the crest of the highest wave. They date back at least to ancient Atlantis and Mu. At all times there have been on earth those who grasped the essentials of spiritual verity. But it is only under conditions like the present, in which the structures erected by self-interest fall and the margins of our earth are washed by the surge of some upper octave planet, that the seeds of wisdom have a chance to grow. Yet even when so germinated and permitted to flourish, history reveals that after a time their precious vegetation has always been turned back under the black soil of material conceptions by the ruthless plough of greed for power and lust for gold.

The sacred wisdom, which even in Atlantis was not so united to material science and mechanical invention as many suppose, cannot be forced upon anyone. Those who adopt any advanced conception must have minds sufficiently educated to understand it. History records, for instance, that Seleucus of Seleuca, a Chaldean, adopted the hypothesis of Aristarchus of Samos and advanced new arguments to support it. He showed that the sun is the center of our system, that the earth has a double motion, revolving around the sun and spinning on its own axis, and he explained the tides, which no doubt he had observed in the Persian Gulf, by referring them to the phases of the Moon. Seleucus lived in the second century B.C., when the intellectual level of the people and the interests of the aristocracy were such that he could not get his ideas accepted. Copernicus had never heard of him; yet 1600 years later he set forth the same ideas. Even then, conditions for their reception were none too favorable, as Galileo found after still another hundred years, when compelled to recant at the hands of the Inquisition.

It is not because wisdom has been absent from the earth that people have wallowed in misconceptions; but that people's minds have been closed to its reception by those in power, whom true spiritual doctrines would rob of their selfish advantages. It is probable that the skill of those more ancient, where material science is concerned, has been exaggerated. Yet we cannot, of course, determine from the excavated public libraries of Chaldea either the extent of their learning nor the opinions of the initiates.

It is the common custom, even in these United States, to remove from public libraries books which do not meet with popular approval, as many know who have donated astrological books, a month or two later to find they have disappeared. But a vast amount of material, written on bricks in cuneiform, has been unearthed and translated, mainly by Strassmaer and Kugler; and from these we are able to judge quite definitely the extent of the knowledge possessed by the official priests at different periods.

The Bible states that Abraham came from Ur, in the land of the Chaldees. The Sumerians were the earliest civilized people in the region; and only a few years ago, near the mouth of the Euphrates, was unearthed a temple belonging to the First Dynasty of Ur. It was conceded to be the oldest Sumerian temple then known. Yet from this ancient Sumerian temple has been recovered a small plaque on which is carved in relief the figure of a manheaded bull with a lion-headed eagle perched on its back. Thus at a time as old as the most ancient civilization of Egypt, we find in use the emblems of the four fixed signs of heaven.

This was the oldest Sumerian temple known up to the commencement of the Pluto period. But since 1930 and the discovery of Pluto, much further north, at Tepe Gawra, excavation has been uncovering successive occupational levels of a mound rising 70 feet above the level of the plain, the latest occupation of which is older than the time of Moses. The mound represents a total of 23 successive levels of occupation, the lowest uncovered at the time of this writing being Level 16. Level 6 down is contemporaneous with the first Dynasty of Ur and the mentioned temple and astrological emblems. Only a few feet below this marks the beginning of recorded history, signalized by the invention of writing. The structures of Level 12 down, some 1,000 years before the beginning of recorded history, were among the earliest buildings of any kind known to archaeology. At Level 13 down, which dates more than 6,000 years ago, was unearthed the oldest temple now known. It is of advanced architecture, and the pottery motives and engraved seal stamps show not merely skill, but true artistic talent.

What astounded the University of Pennsylvania professors in charge of the work was that at such antiquity there were neither mud huts nor crude methods of life. As they stated it: "Those inhabitants of Level 13 were neither primitive nor normal; they were an abnormally gifted and wonderfully balanced people. And they left ample evidence of their achievements in more than one aspect of common life." It seems probable that this advanced culture at so early a date was an inheritance from colonists who brought with them The Religion of the Stars from still more ancient Atlantis.

Some archaeologists argue that before the era of Nebonassar, which adopted a precise solar calendar in 747 B.C., because the popular method of reckoning was a lunar calendar which had little to recommend it, the prediction of periodic astronomical phenomena was impossible. But the same thing might quite as well be said of our miserable Daylight Saving Time which so jumbles up present day chronology.

What the cuneiform libraries reveal, are the records and generally accepted practices of the ruling priesthood. These, backed by their armies, determined what should, and what should not, find its way into the libraries. And even in America today, while from the larger libraries a good grasp of the material sciences might be had, reference to the ancient spiritual teachings is so scant that one looking for evidence of our culture would probably pass it by unnoticed. They would conclude the conceptions of our culture were those of the prevalent orthodox religions.

The conquest of Babylon in 745 B.C. by the Assyrian, Tilgath Pilser, who is mentioned in the Bible, seems to have broken the retarding influence of the orthodoxy of that day, and astronomical precision rapidly developed. It is from this time that the record of the eclipses began which Ptolemy used, and which are sometimes employed by men of science of the present day to test their lunar theories. One of the series is noted in Ptolemy's Almagest and in a cuneiform tablet. The oldest is dated March 21, 721 B.C. Another tablet, dated 523 B.C., shows the relative positions of sun and moon, the precise dates of the conjunctions of the moon with the planets and of the planets with each other, with their positions in the signs of the zodiac; all in advance. That is, there was an advance ephemeris showing planetary positions and phenomena, such as we now use.

From this date to 8 B.C., which is the latest cuneiform document known, there are some fifty documents, all of which have been deciphered, showing progress in precision of astronomical knowledge. The most perfect example dated to the end of the second century B.C., the period in which Posidonius lived. So high a degree of precision was attained that the tables deciphered by F. X. Kugler revealed to him a mistake which had been introduced into, and perpetuated in, the calculations of modern astronomers. The old notations of the Chaldeans have allowed a correction of the canons of Oppolzer.

Commendable as such advanced knowledge of astronomy is, it is not essential to sound astrological practice. As all the major progressed aspects for the life of an individual can be ascertained by direct observation during the 100 days after his birth, and all the minor progressed aspects can be ascertained by direct observation during the 100 months after birth, the most essential data for astrology can be ascertained by such direct observation. And as revealed by the cuneiform records, astronomy then was studied solely for astrological purposes. Thus were the observed positions of the heavenly bodies, together with the events which coincided or which followed, painstakingly recorded in Chaldea for a period of at least 3,000 years.

From the earliest cuneiform inscriptions there was a constant insistence that the things which happen on earth are parallel to the movements and positions in the sky. Not later than 1500 B.C., the vast series of astrological observations made in the past were collected into the Anu-Enlil (Heaven-Earth) series and became the standard astrological reference library. Yet in spite of such complete records, it was not until the dominant corrupt priesthood began to lose its grip that we find the commencement of that marvelous scientific and religious advancement which culminated with Posidonius at the end of the second century B.C.

The rebellion against the priesthood that commenced with the era of Nebonassar in 691 B.C. resulted in Sennacherib of Assyria destroying the holy part of the city Babylon. His son found it expedient to restore these priests to power, and Assurbanipal brought no action against them. But Nabonidus, who followed him, sought their overthrow. The priests of Bel, however, entered into a league with the Persians, and the soldiers of Cyrus entered Babylon without a fight. In gratitude, Cyrus restored the Jews to Jerusalem and the priests of Bel to power. But the plans of these iniquitous priests went astray, as a rebellion broke forth and another Persian, Darius, who had no alliance with them, pulled down the walls of Babylon in 520 B.C.

Already I have mentioned the precision attained in astronomy at this period, as revealed by tables dated 523 B.C. But it should not be thought that the populace, so long kept in darkness by the old grafting priests, had any knowledge of this, or had greater religious freedom.

In Greece, however, there was developing that freedom of thought which, so long as it lasted, was to permit the spread of the scientific knowledge of the Chaldeans and even the spiritual teachings of the Chaldean initiates. Pericles, born about 495 B.C., led the democracy of Athens to an appreciation of knowledge and beauty. He was assisted by Aspasia, a learned woman from Asia Minor, whom Athenian law made it impossible for him to marry.

"Anaxagoras, a stranger welcomed to Athens by Pericles, was saying the strangest things about the sun and stars, and hinting not obscurely that there were no gods, but only one animating spirit in the world."

Following Chaldean instructions, Thales, even before the time of Pericles, had predicted an eclipse; and Plato, born 427 B.C., in his Epinomis, shows clearly the influence of the Chaldean stellar religion. This Chaldean influence, even over the popular mind, was strong enough after the fourth century B.C. that the ancient Greek names of the planets were no longer used, and those of the stellar religion to the east were substituted. Religious intolerance, however, continued a menace to Pericles and to those who came later. The people still clung to their ancient gods.

In America we find evolution to be accepted almost unanimously by scientific men. Yet as late as 1925 the religious prejudices of the less enlightened made itself felt in the famous Scopes trial in which it was made illegal to teach this doctrine in the public schools of Tennessee. So it was in ancient Chaldea, and so it was in even the most liberal period of Greece or Rome; that which could be given wide publicity must ever be governed by the willingness of the population to give it consideration.

It need occasion no surprise, therefore, that it was only after the conquests of Alexander that The Religion of the Stars could openly be taught. Greek savants of repute—Epigenes of Byzantium, Appolonius of Mydnus, Artemidorus of Parium, and others—declared themselves disciples of the Chaldeans, and boasted of being instructed in their schools. Pliny says of Hipparchus, taught by a Chaldean named Kinedas, and proclaimed the founder of modern scientific astronomy, who witnessed the ruin of Babylon: "Hipparchus will never receive all the praise he deserves, since no one has better established the relationship between man and the stars, or shown more clearly that our souls are particles of heavenly fire."

Babylon, captured by the Parthians about 140 B.C., sacked and burned in 125 B.C., was never to regain her splendor. No longer, therefore, could those who sought initiation find it in Chaldea. Yet the knowledge of the Chaldean initiates was not lost; and through the efforts of Posidonius, born at Apamea, in Syria, The Religion of the Stars, for a time released from orthodox suppression, was taught in detail to the Western World. This Master was born about 135 B.C. After long travels he settled in the island of Rhodes, whither his teachings attracted large numbers of Greeks and Romans. Ideas which more than 1,200 years earlier in Egypt Akhenaten had been compelled to express through poetry and the symbolism of art, because his subjects were ignorant of science, could now be set forth by Posidonius in terms of mathematics, mechanics and a philosophy suited to trained minds. It was to be expected that ultimately religious bigotry would destroy all he wrote. But rulers of the world were proud to attend his lectures, and these have preserved in writing the gist of his teachings. From Rome came Pompey and Cicero to sit at his feet.

Then, as now, there was a school of atheistic materialism. The Epicureans taught that the soul was composed of atoms and dissolved with the body. And throughout the Roman Empire the authority of Posidonius, who believed in the immortality of the soul, was set against that of Epicurus. Launching an attack against the Epicureans, he held that their materialistic doctrines were the direct result of their dissolute lives. Rebuking Epicurus for his astronomical fallacies he adds: "No wonder, for to discover the real nature of things is not the part of men devoted to pleasure, but to those whose virtuous characters make the Good their ideal, and who prefer it to the comforts of their beloved flesh."

In the science of his day, rather than by the use of electrons and the principle of radio reception, he taught each branch of The Religion of the Stars set forth in The Brotherhood of Light lessons. A historian, who is a materialist and believes that all beyond the physical is superstition, sums up the 84 years of his life in these words:

> Brought up on Plato and Aristotle, he was equally versed in Asiatic astrology and demonology. He made all human knowledge conspire to the building up of a great system, the coping of which was enthusiastic adoration of the God which permeates the universal organism.
>
> In this vast syncretism all superstition, popular or sacerdotal, soothsaying, divination, magic, find their place and their justification; but above all it was due to him that astrology entered into a coherent explanation of the world, acceptable to the most enlightened intellects, and that it was solidly based on a general theory of nature, from which it was to remain henceforth inseparable.

Mathematics was so closely related to astrology that Mathemaisi in Latin became the synonym for Chaldaei. These astrologers of the Roman Empire laid great stress upon the purity of their morals; they were not merely fortune-tellers, but ministers of The Religion of the Stars. Of the Caesars, Augustus as well as Tiberius was converted to this religion, and many of the later princes adopted it. Yet human nature being what it is, it was not to be expected that the exalted doctrines of Posidonius would indefinitely remain free from the warping influence of self-interest. The Sun, as we know, is the astrological ruler of kings. How easy, therefore, to pervert such knowledge, as in 274 Aurelian did, into official worship of the Sun as the protector of sovereign and empire; the next step, of course, being to proclaim the ruler as the authoritative representative of the Sun on earth, thus establishing the divine right of kings to rule.

Thus did the last vestige of political liberty vanish, and with it religious freedom. Diocletian persecuted the Christians. Then came the Emperor Constantine, who embraced Christianity. And following him another autocrat, Theodosius I, of whom history records:

"He forbade the unorthodox to hold meetings, handed over all the churches to the Trinitarians, and overthrew the heathen temples throughout the empire, and in 390 A.D. he caused the great statue of Serapis at Alexandria to be destroyed. There was to be no rivalry, no qualification, to the rigid unity of the Church."

Posidonius, more than any other, was responsible for the spread of The Religion of the Stars from Chaldea into Europe. This was made possible by the intellectual and religious freedom of his day, an intellectual and religious freedom which it is to be hoped the whole world can enjoy in the near future. If the seeds of spiritual wisdom are to bring forth a bounteous harvest, they must be afforded a suitable soil in which to grow.

Itzamna, Great Initiate of the Mayas

esearchers in Guatemala and Mexico are fast bringing to light convincing evidence that the same brilliant illumination of ancient truth which gave immortal glory to the reign of Akhenaten in Egypt, and which shown so resplendantly later that it enabled Posidonius markedly to influence the intellectual and spiritual trends of Europe, also blazed quite as powerfully, not for the period of one man's life or reign, but for a thousand years over the history of the whole Mayan empire.

No one as yet can prove definitely where this people came from. Their own traditions hold that they came from some region in the sea to the east; but why they came is not in evidence. Their ancestors, no doubt, had their origin in Atlantis or Mu; but these ancient lands had sunk thousands of years before the Mayas arrived in the last land of their adoption. Certainly they did not wander about on the open sea from 9000 B.C. until a hundred years before the commencement of the Christian era.

As yet we do not know from whence they came to Guatemala and the Yucatan; but their own account tells of their leader, who piloted them to safety, taught them writing, architecture, agriculture, astrology and the civilized arts and kept them faithful to The Religion of the Stars for a thousand years, until a foreigner, through military power, gained dominance over them. The name of the great Mayan initiate, whom they held to be a white man, was Itzamna.

The Spaniards, when they arrived, took great pains to destroy the Mayan libraries, so that the details of their history and of The Religion of the Stars as they observed it are lacking. Yet on their stone monuments, which the Spaniards could not destroy, we have the precise dates of the chief events and practices covering a period of about 1,500 years. During this time only two names stand out as of unusual and universal significance. One is that of Itzamna, the great initiate who led them to safety and gave them their arts and religion, and the other is that of the black-bearded Toltec military leader, Kukulcan, who, after inter-tribal wars had weakened them, imposed his will, crushed out the pure practices of The Religion of the Stars, and introduced barbaric Toltec religious customs, including the savage abomination of human sacrifice.

Here we have, on the American continent, an example of the contention of the two ancient forces which gave Atlantis and Mu their glory and which when the constructive element was defeated, ultimately sank them. A thousand years of light, of joy, of happiness and of constructive effort by the Mayan people; and then the forces of darkness, of cruelty and of greed gained the victory and there was quick intellectual and spiritual decay.

Fewer details are known about Mayan history than about the Aztecs for two distinct reasons:

When the Spanish invaded Mexico and Central America, their priests sought out all the books and consigned them to the flames. They also attempted to destroy all monuments and records which might shed any light upon the religion and customs of the people they had conquered.

In the case of the Aztecs, however, almost forty books or manuscripts were smuggled out of the country, were copied, or through other means escaped the vigilance of the Spanish priests and survive to this day. But Bishop Diego de Landa was more successful in suppressing the ancient wisdom of the Mayans.

The Mayas, at the time, had a national library of literature, of science and of history in the form of books written in their hieroglyphic characters, as de Landa records. The national library, and the books in various cities of the empire were not available to the public, but only to the Mayan priests and rulers, who were greatly esteemed for their wisdom.

The books were written and painted on a paper of fiber composition coated with stucco, which made exquisite art work possible. De Landa had a systematic search made of the entire Mayan nation for all such books, gathered them in a great pile in the public square of Mani, and burned them while the populace looked on, powerless to prevent this atrocious vandalism.

Thus of all the Mayan books, invaluable treatises on their beliefs and sciences, only three escaped, no one knows how, and persist to this day. They are: The Peresianus Codex now at the Biblioteque National, Paris; the Dresden Codex, now at the Royal Library at Dresden; and the Tro-Cortesianus Codex, now at the Royal Academy of History, Madrid. Parts of the Tro-Cortesianus appeared in two different countries, and each for a long time was believed to be a separate book. They are now considered as halves of the same book. Perhaps some soldier in pillage tore the book in two and gave one half to his buddy, both parts being smuggled to Europe as souvenirs.

Then again, the Aztecs, in addition to ideographs, used phonetic writing. Ninety per cent of their characters are known, so that such records as are still left in the Aztec language have largely been translated. But the Mayan people used only ideographs, such as we commonly refer to as symbolical pictographs, just a step removed from the simplest of all pictographs. There are 400 basic elements, and about half as many more compound characters; and up to the present time only enough work has been done on these hieroglyphics to make about fifty percent translations.

Yet even as the calendar stone of the Aztecs further north was too ponderous to be destroyed, and was buried by the Spaniards to get rid of it, so the vast cities of Yucatan and Guatemala, with their carvings in stone, were so extensive that their records could not be erased. Each year new cities are discovered, and new information gained, about the highly civilized people who dwelt after the beginning of the Christian era in Southern Mexico and Central America. If their history is ever fully recovered it will reveal, no doubt, much about the most remarkable of all initiates to set foot on American soil. Itzamna taught his people not only architecture the equal of any to be found in the Old World, a hieroglyphic written language, and an unshakable belief in astrology, but even taking into consideration the precision of the Egyptians, Chaldeans and Greeks of that time, a knowledge of astronomy unrivaled anywhere in the whole world.

As to a still earlier occurrence, thousands of years before Itzamna brought his followers to the land that became theirs, the Tro-Cortesianus Manuscripts record:

In the year 6 Kan, on the 11 Muluc, in the month of Zac, there occurred terrific earthquakes which continued until the 13 Chuen without interruption. The country of the hills of earth—the land of Mu (some translate it as Atlantis)—was sacrificed. Twice upheaved, it disappeared during the night, having been constantly shaken by the fires of the underneath. Being confined, these caused the land to rise and sink several times in various places. At last the surface gave way and the ten countries were torn asunder and scattered. They sank with their 64,000,000 inhabitants 8,060 years before the writing of this book.

Although details are lacking, as I said, every stone and monument covering a period of a thousand years in which the hieroglyphics of the Maya are yet to be seen evinces a high knowledge of, and devotion to, The Religion of the Stars. Nearly every such inscription relates to some phenomenon in the sky and the corresponding event which took place on earth. They had worked out a mathematical system which enabled them to predict eclipses and other astronomical phenomena with precision. Much of their chronological data is as yet undeciphered; but their calendar had been adjusted with such nicety that it was superior in accuracy to the Julian Calendar, which was in use in Europe at the same time. The dates of the monuments on which they are engraved are precise enough that no confusion exists between any two days within a period of 370,000 years.

This does not mean, of course, that their dated events go back any such vast period of time. But it does mean that from some source they had obtained a superior knowledge of astronomy. Their oldest date, in which this people gave each consecutive day its own number so that the subsequent records are complete, as worked out by Dr. Spinden of Harvard, is August 6, 613 B.C. The oldest object actually dated is a little jadite figurine known as the Tuxtla statuette, after the place where it was found, bearing the inscription in Mayan chronology, May 16, 98 B.C. However, still older dates are implied.

One of their most inviolate sacred customs was to set up in the various cities, amid a pompous ceremony, a date stone every 1,800 days. When we moderns shall have discovered the exact significance of their Venus calendar, we shall have learned important facts at present unrecognized in reference to mundane astrology. A "tun" is the Mayan year of 360 days. Five "tuns" make up a "hotun" of 1,800 days, and marks the time on which a stone monument was erected bearing the date and recording the most important event of the past period. So prevalent was this custom of setting up date stones at the end of each "hotun" that in their search when archaeologists have been unable to find a certain date stone in any important city, they have felt certain in predicting its existence, and in searching for it until found.

The oldest of these date stones was discovered in 1928 in Uaxactun, and bears the date 97 A.D. The Maya also had a cycle of about 400 years which appeared on the date stones. This oldest date stone bears the record that it is the 8th cycle of the Maya. Dr. Martinez concludes that somewhere in their history, before coming to this place, they had seven previous cycles, commencing with 3113 B.C. At present, however, any date earlier than May 16, 98 B.C. is inferential.

Itzamna, who led them from the region of the rising sun, was not only a benevolent ruler and wise legislator, but so skilled was he in Stellar Healing, even reviving the so-called dead, that he was called Kabul, meaning 'the skillful hand.'

Not always were the followers of Itzamna who lived after his death free from militant aggression which sought to displace both their temporal power and their religion. It was the custom of conquerors not to destroy the older pyramid temples, but to fill their interiors with rubble and then, using the older structures as so much work already done, to build a new pyramid around and over it, leaving no outward trace of the older edifice whose memory and religious implications they wished to efface. A mound near Guatemala City excavated by Dr. A. V. Kidder has disclosed that it contains a series of no less than four superimposed pyramids, indicating a succession of political changes and religious conflicts there. But as a rule there is only one superimposed pyramid, that used by the conquerors of the New Empire established by Kukulcan to conceal the more spiritual doctrines of Itzamna's followers.

Thus at Uaxactun, in Guatemala, by digging into a pyramid a smaller and older pyramid was found inside, that was already an edifice before the Mayan date stone of 97 A. D. was erected. This Itzamna pyramid, some 25 feet high, had been sheathed by a later people to make a pyramid 50 feet high, with a platform on top painted red where the priests stood during sacred ceremonies. This new pyramid served admirably as an astronomical observatory. Three temples were built near it in such a manner that the days of the solstices and equinoxes could be determined from them. When the sun rose behind the northern front corner of the first temple, the observer on top of the pyramid knew it was the summer solstice, June 22. When the sun rose exactly behind the middle of the second temple the equinoxes were at hand, March 21 or September 23. And when the sun rose from the southern front of the third temple it was the day of the winter solstice, December 22.

The most impressive of all the pyramid temples is the great structure of El Castillo, at Chichen Itza, Yucatan. In 1926, Earl Morris, in charge of uncovering this edifice, had almost completed his work when a sculptured column block projecting from a corner of the supporting pyramid suggested to him that some exploratory excavations of this pyramid should be undertaken. And he found that a still older temple had been incorporated in its entirety in the base of the Warrior Temple he had been excavating. Driving tunnels in the Warrior Temple disclosed the stairway and chambers of the older temple, and at the foot of the newly discovered stairway was a skeleton and a rectangular limestone box approximately two and a half feet long, two feet wide, and two feet deep, covered with a stone lid. When the lid was raised the delighted archaeologists found in the box two turquoise mosaic plaques; three necklaces, one of coral, one of turquoise, and one of jade; seven heads of jade; other articles and five jade pendants, one of which was an exquisitely carved iridescent piece representing the figure of Itzamna. The Warrior Cult who paid veneration to Kukulcan, when they hid the temple of Itzamna under an edifice of their own, buried this box containing an image of Itzamna and other articles of the older worship at the foot of the more ancient stairway they covered. Yet, through the diligence of the Mexican government, the interior of this older temple now is open to public inspection.

During the time of Itzamna the people all looked to him for instructions. Their records clearly show that the religion was monotheistic, strictly the worship of a single all-pervading benevolent intelligence who, because he was immaterial was never portrayed by picture or symbol. He was called Hunal-Ku, the One and Only God. The priests of this benevolent Deity looked to the positions of the heavenly bodies to give them information which should guide their affairs. They taught purity of thought and action, exalted deeds of kindness and helpfulness, were averse to war and bloodshed, and urged their people to cultivate the arts. They believed in the power of divination and, according to their own belief, were expert astrologers. At least we know from the Spaniards that Chilan, Balam, and others, foretold the coming of the Whites and the downfall of their empire.

Wherever he gained his knowledge, it seems that Itzamna was fully conversant with The Religion of the Stars in all its branches, and was successful in getting the people whom he led to live according to its precepts. When a new city was established, therefore, in the fifth century by the tribe which called itself Itza, after this initiate, it was named Chichen Itza in his honor.

But after hundreds of years of the religion taught by Itzamna there came Indian tribes from the west, driven by scarcity of food, seeking relief from starvation. The Mayas gave them aid and permitted them to till the land close to Chichen Itza, their greatest city. Later these Tutul-Xius, whom the Mayas had befriended, combined with other Indians and some disgruntled Mayan groups in a war which, about 642 A.D., drove the inhabitants of Chichen Itza from their city into the desert. They were not allowed to return until about 987 A.D.

Although they recovered their city, other Mayan groups and Indian tribes were still hostile. Thus arose, through internal strife, the opportunity for a statesman of sagacity and power, who came from the west across the Mexican Gulf, to gain complete dominance over their thoughts and customs. The black-bearded Toltec, Kukulcan, called a meeting of the various kings, elected one of the old Itzas emperor, and formed in 1027, the League of Mayapan. This league was successful for a time in suppressing intertribal warfare, but the temporary peace it brought was purchased at an enormous price. The soldiers of Kukulcan thrust to one side the incorporeal God of Itzamna and substituted the many Toltec gods; and there came into vogue, instead of the harmless and devout ceremonies of the old Mayan priests, the vicious rites and gruesome practices of Toltec religion. Even as Itzamna, coming with his followers from the East, betokened the rise of Mayan spirituality, so the establishment of the New Empire by Kukulcan, coming from the West, and the superimposing of the Warrior Temples over the older ones, heralded the setting of the spiritual sun.

When Kukulcan grew old and his powers began to fail, he yearned for leisure, and about the year 1087 he again embarked to sail across the Mexican Gulf, leaving the port by which he entered, never to return. The confederation of states due to his genius persisted until about 1200 A.D., and then, as was sure to happen sooner or later, again broke up into warring tribes and kingdoms. It was this bloody strife, continuing over a period of more than three hundred years, which reduced the Mayas to a state of helplessness that made their conquest by the Spaniards an easy matter. The last of their 1,800 day date stones was erected in 1541, and the following year they were conquered by the Spanish and such knowledge as their priests yet possessed was destroyed.

Although, like other things of earth, the knowledge and spirituality of the Maya proved impermanent, and although only an outline rather than the details of their practices are available, a thousand years of The Religion of the Stars seems to be an honor which excavations now under progress will accord to the influence of Itzamna, Great Initiate of the Mayas.

Stellar Religion of the Pre-Incas

ar to the south of the Mayas, across the Isthmus and in a region much more rugged, were another people of high culture about whom we know still less. Let us consider the year 1531, in the magnificent city of Cuzco, high in the Andes, 500 miles inland from where the Pacific laps the South American shore. There the previous year Pizarro, the Spaniard, had landed, enticed the Inca king Atahualpa into his camp, slaughtered his retinue, and held him for ransom. The price of the king's liberty was a room full of gold. The treasures poured in, hundreds of llama trains were on their way laden with golden temple vessels. But the Spaniards grew impatient, strangled Atahualpa, and the llama trains turned back. Treasures which are still hunted but seldom found, were hidden in caves, buried in secret spots, thrown into the river; anywhere that would deprive the invaders of their spoil.

The Incas, themselves, were an invading ruling class, who after long struggle had gained dominion over a population of ten million. Like the ruling caste in other lands, they looked to the wisdom of the priests for guidance. These priests were custodians of the Stellar Wisdom gained from the Pre-Incas, the older superseded people who left distinctive relics and characteristic walls of stone that yet may be found in various places in the mountains.

The Stellar Wisdom held that gold was the metal of the sun, and that the sun was ruler of the king. Thus to the populace, as is taught in Japan today, the royal family was descended from the sun. As the sun is astrologically supreme, in the capital city, Cuzco, the most magnificent temple was dedicated to it. The roof was of precious woods plated with gold. A six-inch frieze of gold ran outside around the building. The doors opened to the east, and at the far end above the altar was a golden disc with human countenance shaped and graved to represent the sun, and studded with precious stones. It was so located that, at the equinoxes, the rays of the rising sun falling on its polished surface gave a reproduction in the temple of the brilliant source of light.

Around this central edifice where homage was paid to Inti, signifying both sun and light, were smaller astrological temples. Most important of these was one dedicated to the moon, consort of the sun. Instead of gold, its great disc was of silver. Its ornaments and decorations also were of this lunar metal. Still further bespeaking precise astrological knowledge, around the sacred city of the sun were placed twelve great stone columns, on each of which successively the sun was deemed to rest. Even the Incas, the ruling class, were privileged to gain only a portion of the Stellar Knowledge. A priesthood dedicated to the light, and having rigid requirements for initiation, were the custodians of this pre-Inca wisdom, and held many another precious secret.

Not too distant from the temple of the sun stood a magnificent structure which housed the temple virgins. They were high-born girls, selected for their beauty and dedicated to temple service, and like the vestal virgins of ancient Rome, next to the king were the most sacred persons in the land.

This was the setting when the predatory conquistadors, having slain the Inca king, and thus instead of hastening, had turned back the flood of gold, marched into Cuzco. Each mail-clad soldier ripped gold from the temple walls. The great disc of precious metal which served to mirror the equinoctial rising sun became the stake for which the soldiers brawled and gambled. Then, when each had gathered to himself such gold as he could reach, he grabbed a lovely treasure of the flesh. The virgins of the sun were roughly seized, were hunted when they fled, and made the prey of the bestial soldier crew. Not all, however, suffered such degrading fate. One hundred of them vanished, nor all the Spanish search could find a trace of them. They were there, they had gone; and for four hundred years that disappearance was a mystery.

Not only the knowledge of the stars and the spiritual teachings of the constellations, but many another precious secret, was in the custody of the Stellar Priests. Cuzco had not always been the empire's capital. Seven hundred years before, still earlier Peruvians had built a most amazing citadel. Finally abandoned in favor of Cuzco when certain perils had passed, for 200 years it had been forgotten to all except the Stellar Priests, who kept it in repair for secret refuge. It was to this white granite city, over secret trails, that the priests led the 100 fleeing virgins. They gained the 14,000 foot crest of the Continental Divide, and then, for some distance, descended the tropical Urubamba canyon toward the Amazon. Here was a city of 400 hewn-stone houses. The temple was built of irregular, dissimilar, many-joined stones of gigantic size fitted with pre-Inca nicety. One block in it is 14 feet long and 8 feet high.

Machu Picchu, as the city is called, is an incredible place. It is built on a spur, with precipitous sides dropping 2,000 feet all around except for a narrow strip of rock connecting it with the main mountain range. Across this narrow strip was built a stone wall, by which soldiers could protect its only approach. It was the best spot in all the Andes from which to repel invasion. Built 700 years before the fleeing virgins reached its then-deserted houses, outside the wall were small terraced gardens which gave food supply, and limited the old time population to about 9,000.

At the very apex of the place is a stone sun dial three feet in diameter, with a square hub a foot high in the center. This ancient astronomical instrument was called Intihuatana—Inti, meaning sun, and huatana, meaning tied—"The place where the sun is tied." Those who built the city and used this observatory were well versed in stellar lore.

Here, untouched by the outside world, the 100 fleeing temple virgins lived out the span of their lives. Their graves reveal the story. One by one, as the hand of age laid heavily upon them, they died, still inviolate virgins to the sun, leaving no issue. Those surviving performed the last rites until, after scores of years, the last one passed on, with none left to bury her. The Stellar Priests likewise lived out their span of years in this lost city of the mountains. And when they died, they too were gathered to their fathers, taking with them the knowledge of their caste, the priceless Stellar Wisdom.

Only by an archaeological accident was the city ever found. In 1911, nearly four hundred years after the virgins fled the embrace of the mail-clad Spanish soldiers to be seen no more, Machu Picchu, the impregnable city of white granite houses where the sun is tied, was discovered by Professor Hiram Bingham of Yale.

Chapter 5

Astrology of the Aztecs

ne of the objects of imposing interest to visitors to the Century of Progress Fair at Chicago in 1933, was the Aztec Calendar Stone. Quite appropriately it was not in the Fair grounds, for the miserable daylight saving time then in use, and the months of different duration, represented anything but progress over the system of time-recording used by the Aztecs. The cast duplicating the stone is in the Field Museum just outside the north entrance of what was the Fair grounds.

The Calendar Stone, and the calendar pictured directly above it, (see page 40) represent only one of three types of calendars used by the Aztecs. The upper one here pictured was all the general populace needed, for the Aztec year was composed of four seasons of equal length, starting at the time the sun reached the same point of the zodiac each year. The season being known, a glance at this calendar gave the name of the day, and revealed the zodiacal degree occupied by the sun.

Aztec astrologers, however, needed more in their work than the sun's position on a given date. East and west, ancient and modern, astrological practice stressed the importance of the position of the moon as well as that of the sun, and their relation to each other. In natal astrology, for instance, the sign and decanate occupied by the sun show the individuality, and the sign and decanate occupied by the moon indicate the mentality. In horary astrology, especially in selecting the proper time to do something, the aspect of the moon to the sun is most important. For a proposition to have a strong vitality and long lease of life, it should be started in the first quarter of the moon; for quick maturity, just before the full moon. Potatoes should be planted in the dark of the moon, and weeds are killed more easily when the lunar orb is in the last quarter.

Even today a perpetual calendar, showing year after year on what dates the sun and moon will occupy certain signs and when they will repeat any aspect that may be selected, would be an advantage to any astrologer. The more ancient peoples—probably the inhabitants of Atlantis or Mu who colonized the seven ancient centers of civilization, from whom the Chaldeans and Aztecs alike gained their vast astronomical and astrological knowledge—had devised just such a wheel in the form of a swastika. The emblem of the swastika, found on every continent, had its origin in a lunar-solar calendar.

Almost every year astrologers make predictions as to what the eclipses during that year probably foreshow. And to determine this for any particular country, they must know in what house of the chart the eclipse falls. Ancient astrologers also required, for the practice of mundane astrology, to know the dates on which eclipses would take place, and in what houses of the horoscope they would fall. To determine this, as well as to check the swastika calendar at certain intervals, they devised a third form of calendar, the triskelion. But before explaining the use of either the swastika calendar or the triskelion calendar, we should first discuss the popular season calendar and the calendar stone, both of which are illustrated at the commencement of this chapter.

The Popular Season Calendar
The Aztec nation, like the Sumerians of Asia Minor, kept careful records of events and maintained an astronomical department. The statistical method, which the Church of Light Astrological Research Department is so successfully employing, is not a new thing. The astrology of the ancients was founded upon the comparison of the positions of the heavenly bodies with the events which happened.

The Anu-Enlil series, recorded in cuneiform writing, extends back to observations in the valley of the Tigris-Euphrates earlier than 2750 B.C., and is believed to have covered an almost unbroken period of at least a thousand years. The later fame of the Chaldeans was founded upon the accuracy secured through the use of these comparative records. How far back the comparative astrological records of the Aztecs go has not been determined because, with the invasion of Mexico by the Spanish, every effort was made to destroy all records. Don Juan de Zumarraga "collected these historical paintings and records from every quarter." He caused them to be piled in a "mountain heap," as it was called by Spanish writers, and reduced them to a pile of ashes.

But the Calendar Stone was not so easily destroyed. Smaller stone records might be broken up, but this wheel was a mass of basaltic porphyry eleven feet, eight inches in diameter, and weighed some twenty-four tons. Sometime between 1551 and 1559, after the execution of such Aztecs as were known to possess historical or astrological knowledge, Friar Alonso de Montfar had the stone secretly buried. No one suspected its existence for over two hundred years until 1790, when some workmen, excavating in the Plaza Mayor, unearthed this huge testimony of astrological knowledge, and it now rests in the Mexican National Museum.

To understand the use of this stone we must understand the use of the swastika in recording dates. Fortunately there has been bequeathed to us a complete swastika recording wheel, such as the Aztec astrologers used. This complete swastika wheel for determining astronomical positions for any given date was sketched by Diego Duran, and is included in his History of the Indians of New Spain. This was written earlier than 1588, and Duran, who was a native of Tezcoco, paid the penalty for his temerity by being excommunicated and burned alive by the Spaniards.

The four arms of the swastika (see reproduction of Duran's sketch at bottom corner of illustration on page vi) represent the four seasons of the year. Each of the four seasons, commencing with the winter solstice, about December 22, consisted of exactly 91 days. The four seasons, therefore, embraced 364 days; but the Aztec year contained 365¼ days. To allow for this discrepancy, each year had at its end a festival day, and each fourth year contained two festival days, called "enmontemi," or useless days, because on these days no work was done. Each of these four seasons had a name, and was composed of seven weeks of thirteen days each. The names of the four seasons were: 1. Reed. 2. Rabbit. 3. House. 4. Flint Knife.

Historians, both early and late, because they scorn to know anything about astrology and are equally ignorant of universal symbolism, have uniformly made the mistake of considering the twenty pictures of the calendar reproduced at the top of page vi to represent the days of a twenty-day month, there being eighteen such months in a year. It remained for Edward Butt, a civil engineer of accomplishment, the president of the Kansas City Science Club, to show how ridiculous such an assumption is, and to prove conclusively that these twenty pictures are the names of the thirteen days of each week plus the names of the seven weeks of each season. His researches have shown how the common calendar, the swastika calendar, and the triskelion calendar, were used to record and predict astronomical phenomena. This makes it possible for me here to indicate their importance in the astrological practice of the Aztecs.

In the single season calendar—the upper illustration at the commencement of this chapter—the dots in the outer circle adjacent to each picture indicate the picture is that of the first, second, third, and so forth day; or of the first, second, third, and so-on week. Their names are: 1. Crocodile. 2. Wind. 3. House. 4. Lizard. 5. Snake. 6. Death. 7. Deer. 8. Rabbit. 9. Water. 10. Dog. 11. Monkey. 12. Hay. 13. Reed.

After the Reed, opposite which are thirteen dots to indicate it to be the thirteenth day, there is a jaguar, opposite which is one dot, to signify it to be the first week of the season. The names of the seven weeks are: 1. Jaguar. 2. Eagle. 3. Vulture. 4. Sun. 5. Flint. 6. Rain. 7. Flower.

Just as we assume that most people know that Wednesday is the fourth day of the week, and that July is the seventh month of the year, without our placing a number before them to indicate it, so the artisan who made the huge Calendar Stone assumed that it was unnecessary to place the customary dots, representing numbers, opposite the pictures of the thirteen days and seven weeks. Yet in this circle of pictures around the central part of the Calendar Stone are to be seen the same twenty characters, in conventionalized form, that are to be seen in the season calendar reproduced above the Calendar Stone at the head of this chapter.

In the Calendar Stone, however, as you will observe, they start at what in a birthchart represents the tenth house occupied by the first day of the week—the Crocodile—and proceed from this zenith position contra-clockwise, in the directions the planets move through the zodiac in a birthchart, which is also the manner in which the signs of the zodiac follow each other when we face the south, or erect a chart of the heavens as viewed while facing south, which is the way they appear in a birthchart erected for a point north of the equator. That is, they go around in the opposite direction from the other single-season calendar reproduced above the Calendar Stone, which follows an order of succession clockwise around the circle, as the signs of the zodiac follow each other when the observer faces north, this being the order the symbols follow on the north facade of the famous Bok Tower in Florida. Yet in each calendar the fourteenth picture is the jaguar, representing not one of the days, but the first week of the season.

If we wish to designate a certain date, we may say it will fall on the day of the week, Monday, on the eighth day of the month of January, in the year 1934. The Aztecs would say this same date falls on the day of Coatl (serpent), the week of Quauhtl (eagle), in the season of Acatl (reed), in the year designated by the triskelion.

The date thus recorded informs an astrologer—American or Aztec, according to the system used—the degree of the zodiac occupied by the Sun. In this case, the date falling seventeen days after the winter solstice, the Sun is seventeen degrees from this point—its movement being approximately one degree per day— which we call the eighteenth degree of Capricorn.

As I have an ephemeris for 1934 at hand, I can easily determine that the Moon is in Libra, making the last square aspect to the Sun. Yet if I were asked where the Moon will be on some date in 1960 or 1970, I would have to employ the Metonic Cycle, discovered by a Greek named Meton about 433 B.C. It consists of 235 synodic months (from New Moon to New Moon), which quite closely equal 19 common years of 365¼ days. 235 months equal 6939 days, 16 hours, 31 minutes. 19 tropical years (the year commonly used) equal 6939 days, 14 hours, 27 minutes. Thus at the end of 19 years the New and Full Moon recur on the same day of the year, but 2 hours, 4 minutes later in the day. The calendar of the phases of the Moon thus for 1934, 1952 and 1972 are the same, except that intervening leap years may change the dates by one day. From the sign and degree occupied by the Sun on a given day, when the day is indicated as a definite number of days before or after New Moon or Full Moon, it is thus possible to ascertain for any given date in advance of ephemeris publication what sign the Moon will occupy.

However, the number of present-day astrologers who can do this is quite limited. Yet the Aztec astrologer could locate by the triskelion the relation of the Moon to the Sun at the commencement of some year near the date required. Then by counting forward or backward on the swastika calendar from the date so located he could instantly find each day of the year, or any year near it, when the same relation existed between Sun and Moon. That is, he could employ the swastika calendar to do the same work we use the Metonic Cycle to accomplish. The common calendar, just described, enabled him to know the degree of the zodiac occupied by the Sun. Then knowing the distance of the Moon from the Sun on this day of the year, mental arithmetic would indicate just what sign the Moon would occupy on that date.

A photographic reproduction of the Swastika Calendar wheel, as sketched by Diego Duran in his *History of the Indians of New Spain*, a book written before 1588, will be found at the lower left-hand corner of the illustration on page vi. We owe the preservation of this sketch to the desire of those who had Duran executed to keep tangible evidence that their action was justifiable. The drawing of a Swastika Calendar was retained by them as prima facie evidence that the writer had affiliations with the devil. According to historical records, "this second calendar arouses a holy indignation in the early Spanish missionaries, and Father Sahagun loudly condemns it as most unhallowed, since it is founded neither on natural reason, nor on the influence of the planets, nor on the true course of the year; but it is plainly the work of necromancy, and the fruit of a compact with the devil."

The Swastika is not a single season calendar like the Calendar Stone and the other one whose use I have just explained. Instead, it is a calendar for the whole year, each of the four seasons commonly being indicated by a picture of its name. The Swastika Calendar's square compartments each represent one of the thirteen days of the week, the particular day being designated, not by the number of dots in each compartment, as in the season calendar, but by counting clockwise around each swastika arm, commencing with the compartment next to the wheel's hub for the first day. Thus in the illustration at the bottom right-hand corner of page vi, the first day of the week of the first season is represented by 1, the second day by 10, the third day by 6 and the thirteenth day by 5. That each season has seven weeks is indicated by the seven vocal expressions issuing from the mouth of a human face adjacent to each arm of the Swastika. The first day of the second season is at 4, the second day is represented by 13, the fifth day by 1 and the thirteenth day by 8.

The Aztec system of dividing a year into four seasons, each containing seven weeks of thirteen days, is thus represented in this calendar. The thirteen compartments in the upper left-hand arm each have the picture of a reed, representing the first, or Reed, quarter of the year. The thirteen compartments of the upper right-hand arm show a rabbit's picture, indicating the second, or Rabbit, quarter. The thirteen compartments of the lower right-hand arm have a house, picturing the third, or House, quarter of the year, and the thirteen compartments of the lower left-hand arm, show a flint knife, representing the fourth, or Flint Knife, quarter.

Near Mexico City one huge pyramid erected to the Sun and another to the Moon attest the importance placed upon these luminaries by an ancient people. The positions of the Sun and Moon in the zodiac, and the aspects made by them to each other, have ever been considered of prime importance whenever and wherever astrology has been practiced.

The Aztec Swastika Calendar was designed not only to reveal, at any date, the relation of the Sun and Moon to each other and the recurrence of astronomical phenomena, but to indicate also numerical relations and spiritual verities. No student of Ancient Masonry can fail to perceive the significance of the positions occupied by the Sun, Moon and five planets in the Aztec season calendar illustrated at the commencement of this chapter. He will gather that the Sun and Moon as there pictured are symbolic of the relation between man and woman; for the astrologers of ancient times were not interested in conjunctions and other aspects of Sun and Moon merely as astronomical facts, but also as corresponding to the spiritual possibilities of the human soul, and as aiding man to scale the spiritual heights. He will perceive further, that those who designed the Swastika Calendar were aware of the means that must be employed by the soul of every life form, including that of man, to make evolutionary progress. A belief is indicated that all energy, physical, intellectual and spiritual, is the offspring of positive and negative forces, symbolized by Sun and Moon; for the spiral which results is an integral part of the Swastika Calendar.

Consulting either of the Swastika Calendars at the bottom corners of the illustration on page vi, if you will start at the hub with 1 and trace a line through consecutive numbers around the wheel—2, 3, 4, 5, 6, and so on—you will find that the line so formed is a spiral. As that information is already set forth fully in Brotherhood of Light Course IV, *Ancient Masonry*, it will serve no adequate purpose to trace the religious conceptions of the Aztecs further. Students of that course know that such a spiral implies a belief in the evolution of the soul, not merely on earth, but also in the endless vistas of the after-life. As it further indicates the means by which the perpetual progress may be hastened, it is no wonder that Father Sahagun considered the wheel "plainly the work of necromancy."

Midsummer Sunrise and the Ancient Rites of Stonehenge
Now to more clearly indicate the point of departure which the Aztecs used in their calendar system let us temporarily leave America and go to the County of Wiltshire in England. There may be seen the ruins of what is probably the most perfect example of its kind of an ancient temple of the Religion of the Stars. Stonehenge has been reconstructed as a model; and archaeologists are able to furnish a detailed description of its original appearance and structure. Their opinion is that it was built about four thousand years ago.

The history of the region goes back about half that far, only to the time of the Roman conquest. At this much later date Roman history records that the Druid priests taught many things about the size and dimensions of the stars, that they believed the soul of man has previously occupied lower forms of life, and that after death man lives, much as he lives on earth, in some superior region. With such accounts of the beliefs of those still inhabiting the vicinity at the time of the Roman invasion, let us read Stonehenge in terms of its own language, the language of universal symbolism.

The outside of this temple consists of a circular earthwork three hundred feet in diameter. Because the constellations surrounding the zodiac and picturing its influence are composed of an infinite number of stars, such a mound, not distinguished by clearly marked divisions, well represents the surrounding starry firmament.

Immediately within this earthwork originally was a circle of small "foreign stones," the foundations of which only now remain. These "foreign stones" represent the influence of the zodiac and its divisions. Then, interior to these, comes a complete ring of hewn stones with lintels mortised to their tops, making a series of doorways. These doorways, extending completely around the circle, are not made of "foreign stones," because the houses of the birthchart are not dependent upon stellar influences, but upon the position on the earth where such influences fall.

Inside this ring of stone doorways is another ring of "foreign stones," indicating the motion of the planets in their orbits. Within these is a horseshoe of five dolmens. The number five is the symbol of man, and was so considered in all the ancient schools. A dolmen, consisting of two upright stones with a horizontal stone top, is a doorway; the horizontal stone conveying the idea of a higher plane. The five dolmens signify the belief that man passes through the doorway of physical dissolution to continue life and effort in a higher realm.

Within the five dolmens is a horseshoe of "foreign stones." The horseshoe form is the symbol of the feminine in nature, even as the single upright stone is the symbol of the masculine. The crescent is also the symbol of the Moon.

Within the curve of this horseshoe is a flat, horizontal slab of stone serving as an altar. In this temple many different ceremonies were performed, but only one will be mentioned here. The neophyte to be initiated, standing on this slab of stone within the horseshoe at sunrise on the day of the summer solstice, portrayed the age-old mystery of the virgin conception.

In the center of the avenue of approach, and so located that the rising Sun on the longest day of the year sheds its rays directly over it into the horseshoe and upon the altar, is a large, unworked, upright stone, representing the Sun and the masculine in nature.

In nature there is a constructive principle and a destructive principle. Light is the universal symbol of the constructive attribute, while darkness is representative of that which is destructive. At the time of the summer solstice the day is longest, the Sun highest in the heavens. Symbolically, the power of light then reaches its maximum. The neophyte, standing on the altar, as the rising Sun that day sheds its light over the

Sun-stone, represents the soul within the womb of matter, reunited to its divine source by a spiritual ray.

The avenue and its stones indicate the steps he has taken to reach his present illumination. His position reveals his knowledge that physical life is merely a period of gestation, from which he will be born into the life of a more glorious existence. He is surrounded by symbols that represent the mundane houses, the zodiac and the planets, indicating that he recognizes their influence both upon his life here and upon his life on the higher plane, signified by the dolmens.

The "foreign stones" which represent the influence of the zodiac, the circling planets and the crescent Moon, have not been quarried, as were the other stones, in the near vicinity, but to represent their influence coming from afar, have been brought from some distant place.

The neophyte, with the light of the rising Sun shining upon him this longest day of the year, has come into a realization of the meaning of life; that the life below is a preparatory school in which the soul is trained according to the function it is to perform in the universal organization. His soul entered matter to gain this training, and now, as indicated by the rays of the rising Sun reaching him, it is once more consciously united to its ego, to the sun of its divine source. Now and hereafter, astrological forces will play their part. But having arrived at the state of true illumination, he is no longer a neophyte, for he is conscious of his cosmic work.

Commencement of the Aztec Year

People now visit Stonehenge on Mid-summer Day to watch the sunrise at the summer solstice exactly over the "Hele Stone," as it is called. This and the other solstice point are easily determined without delicate instruments, and constitute natural starting points for recording time and astronomical phenomena far better than our first day of January, which is some nine or ten days after the winter solstice. At the summer solstice the shadow cast by a stake at noon, as determined by a tracing in the dust, is shortest. At the winter solstice, the shadow cast by the stake at noon, as determined by tracings in the snow, is longest. Thus to determine these dates is a simple matter.

The power of light reigns supreme at the summer solstice. At the winter solstice the power of darkness is defeated, the stone of the tomb of winter is rolled away, the nights cease growing longer, and there is gift-giving and rejoicing. With this explanation of why the Aztec year commenced at the winter solstice, let us use the Swastika Calendar to determine, Aztec fashion, the recurrence of some particular aspect between Sun and Moon.

One method of procedure is to commence with the relation of the Sun and Moon on the first day of the year, and follow through the year, noting each time the same relation occurs; then from this to determine on just what days the particular aspect reaches a state of perfection. Thus, if the first day of the year was just two days after the New Moon, as determined by observation, each of the days noted would again be two days after the New Moon; and as the Moon moves approximately thirteen degrees a day, the day of the week when any aspect forms can be computed. In this method, it should be noted, there is a shift backward of two days for compensation when entering the fourth season.

Now suppose some aspect, no matter which one, occurs between Sun and Moon on the first day of the year. This first day of the year is represented by 1 in the upper left-hand arm of the swastika. Call this the starting point, and make two complete circuits and a fraction in the direction of the faint dotted tracing in the Swastika Calendar at the lower right-hand corner of the illustration on page vi until, as shown by the arrow, you arrive at 2. Two is the fourth day from 1, and as two and a fraction circuits of the thirteen day week have been made, the second time the aspect is made is on the fourth day of the third week of the first season.

Then commencing at 2, make two more complete circuits and a fraction, until you arrive at 3. As 3 is the seventh day from 1, and as four and a fraction circuits have been made, the third time the aspect occurs is on the seventh day of the fifth week of the first season. Making two and a fraction circuits more brings you to 4, indicating that the fourth time the aspect occurs is on the tenth day of the seventh week of the first season of the year.

Now as there are three days remaining to complete the seven circuits of the first season—13, 9, 5—in starting the second season you count ahead three—4, 13, 9—and call 9 (A) the starting point for reckoning the second season. Two and a half circuits from this point brings you to 5. As 5 is the second day removed from the starting point (A), and as two and a half circuits have been made, it indicates that the fifth time the aspect occurs in the year is on the second day of the third week of the second season.

Following this system, and bearing in mind the carrying over of the days into the next season, when this transition occurs, one can calculate, on the Swastika Calendar, the period of recurrence for any given luminary aspect. But to predetermine the proper starting point for calculating the days on which a given aspect between Sun and Moon will occur requires something else. The something else which was employed by the Aztecs was:

The Triskelion Calendar
Historians, only because they are ignorant of universal symbolism, have tried to explain the calendar shown in the upper right-hand corner of the illustration on page vi as representing the 18 weeks of 20 days each in the Aztec year. Plainly shown in the center is a picture of the Sun, with its rays extending outward. Covering a portion of the Sun is a New Moon. The only time the Moon covers the Sun's face is when an eclipse takes place. The only time there is an eclipse of the Sun is when a New Moon occurs, which, as soon as new, has the crescent appearance shown in this picture.

As it is obviously the picture of a solar eclipse, why try to make anything else out of it? The eighteen symbols around the outside of the figure are thus proclaimed to relate to eclipses. As eclipses occur under almost the same conditions after 18 years, 11 and one-third days (18 years, 10 and one-third days when five leap years instead of four intervene), it is evident that these 18 symbols are the names of each year in the eclipse period. This period of 18 years, 11 and one-third days was called the Saros by the Chaldeans, who used it in predicting eclipses. It is highly probable that the Aztecs gained their knowledge of this period from the same ancient source as did the Chaldeans. The period, according to modern astronomers, is remarkable from the fact that after this elapse of time the Moon has passed through perigee 239 times, and is almost exactly the same distance from the earth as at start, as well as being at the same phase and same distance from a node. That is, almost the same conditions recur as affecting New Moons and eclipses.

Again applying universal symbolism to the picture, we find that the symbols are grouped by threes, suggesting that each symbol is, in some manner, to be used three times. If each symbol represents a year of the eclipse period, and all are repeated three times, we have a still larger period of 54 years.

As the Saros, or 18 year period, contains a fraction of a day—to be precise it is 18 years, 11 days, 7 hours, 42 minutes—the eclipse that takes place after such a lapse of time does not occur at the same place. That is, if the first eclipse took place on the midheaven of a map for a given place, the eclipse after an eighteen year period would probably occur below the western horizon. But after three of these Saros periods, the eclipse would occur again in almost the same heavenly position it did the first time, and its shadow would be observed in practically the same place on the surface of the earth. That is, if it took place on the midheaven once, 54 years, 33 days later it would take place 13½ degrees east of the midheaven, or just about in the middle of the tenth house.

The Chaldeans had a still larger period, called Naros, which consisted of 600 years. This period is supposed to bring the Sun, Moon and naked-eye planets back to the same zodiacal degree they occupied, on the same day of the year, every 600 years. If this period is as perfect as has been claimed by some astronomers, it would be possible for a birthchart to repeat, and except for the influence of the upper octave planets, similar characters to be born at 600 year intervals. However, the fixed stars would have shifted relative to the zodiac a little over 8 degrees. I mention this merely to indicate that in the valley of the Tigris-Euphrates still larger periods of time were made use of than the "bundle of years" consisting of 54 years, 33 days, which constituted the equivalent of century to the Aztecs.

As we reckon time from a given point as being in the first century or second century, so the Aztecs reckoned time as being in the first bundle of years, second bundle of years, and so on. The commencement of a "bundle of years" was easily ascertained by observation; for at that time an eclipse of the Sun would be visible in some predetermined region of the heavens.

The Saros periods were named after the first year, second year and third year of each period. Each of the 18 years had a name. These names translated mean: 1. Want of Water. 2. Boning of Men. 3. Short Feast. 4. Long Feast. 5. Dry. 6. Porridge. 7. Little Feast. 9. Birth of Flowers. 10. Fall of Fruit. 11. Time of Bloom. 12. Arrival of the Gods. 13. Feast of the Mountains. 14. Bird. 15. Feast of the

Flags. 16. Fall of Waters. 17. Severe Weather. 18. Resuscitation.

Thus the seventh year of the first Saros was called the year Tecuilhuitonth, of the period (Saros) Atacahualco (Want of Water). The ninth year of the second Saros was called the year Tlaxochimaco of the period (Saros) Tlacxipehualiztli (Boning of Men). And the fourteenth year of the third Saros was called the year Quecholli of the period (Saros) Tozozontli (Short Feast).

The Aztecs kept accurate records of all celestial phenomena, including eclipses and New Moons. That they observed the positions of the five naked-eye planets and made use of them in their predictions is evident from the pictures of these planets occupying so prominent a place in the single season calendar reproduced at the commencement of this chapter. But the knowledge of just how they handled these other five orbs, and made use of them in their astrology seems to have perished in the flames of the "mountain heap" of documents and historical records so assiduously collected by Don Juan de Zumarraga. How they ascertained New Moons and eclipses, however, and were able to predict their zodiacal and birthchart positions far in advance, is set forth by these calendars we are discussing.

Eclipses occur at frequent intervals. In fact, there are always two solar eclipses and there may be as many as five, during a single calendar year. Some years there are no lunar eclipses, but in other years there are two; so that at rare intervals as many as seven eclipses occur in a single calendar year. There can never be more than three lunar eclipses in a year. In a single Saros period there are usually about seventy eclipses, varying two or three, one way or the other, as new eclipses come in at the eastern limit and go out at the western. Of the 70 about 29 are lunar and 41 solar. Of the solar eclipses, which are considered to be of much greater importance both by the Aztecs and by modern astrologers, approximately 27 are central, 17 being annular and 10 total. Yet although somewhere on the earth there are about 10 total eclipses in 18 years, as the shadow of totality averages less than 100 miles in width, it covers only about $\frac{1}{200}$ of the earth's surface. This means that any given locality on the earth will be in the path of the total shadow in the long run only about once in 360 years.

An eclipse of the sun can take place only at new moon and an eclipse of the moon can take place only at full moon. Such eclipses could be predicted, not only as to date but as to the certainty that the shadow would or would not fall on Mexico, and that it would occur in a certain area of the sky which we call a given mundane house, by the Aztecs. But it should not be thought that they, or the Chinese or the Chaldeans, attained anything like the precision our modern astronomers attain in predicting these or other astronomical phenomena.

An eclipse of the sun usually is not coincident with new moon, although in astrology the new moon or full moon which is an eclipse gives the time for erecting the chart and the degree and minute used for ascertaining the influence of the eclipse. Although the new moon and the eclipse are never more than a few minutes apart, an eclipse of the sun is the relation of the moon's shadow to the surface of the earth. To determine the moment of eclipse at a given place on the earth where it is visible, the moon's parallax must enter into the calculation. The moon's parallax is the angular distance from the earth's center the point on the earth under consideration is as viewed by an imaginary observer on the moon. The computation of the various elements of a solar eclipse to outline its shadow and its time not only was far beyond the ability of the ancients, but thus to compute these factors of one total solar eclipse requires that a mathematician, with all modern tables available, who is skilled in astronomical calculations, put in about 120 hours of close and exacting work.

The word Saros means "repetition," referring to the fact that an eclipse phenomena repeat after the interval indicated by this period. In reference to solar eclipses the chief difference between two eclipses separated by one Saros is the location of the path of the moon on the surface of the earth, the second eclipse falling some 115½ degrees further west than the first one, and some 200 miles farther north or south.

The moon in its orbit around the earth does not follow the same path the sun apparently does. Instead, the orbit of the moon is at an angle of about 5 degrees to the ecliptic, or path of the sun, so that when the sun and moon are exactly in the same degree of the zodiac and thus the same in east-west position, they may still be several degrees apart in north-south position. And as the diameter of the sun or moon is only about half a degree, the effect, so far as the shadow is concerned, is as if an object were slightly west of a building in the morning, but ten times the width of the building to the north or south of it; that is, in spite of any east-west relation, the shadow of the building could not touch it. And thus it is also when the moon is much north or south of the path of the sun at either new moon or full moon.

The nodes are the places where the path of a planet cuts the ecliptic, or apparent path of the sun. The orbits of all the planets, including the moon, have nodes; for they are inclined to the plane of the ecliptic. When the moon reaches either its north node (Dragon's Head) or south node (Dragon's Tail) it is neither north nor south of the path of the sun, and when it is thus a few degrees from either of these nodes it is only a little to the north or south of the path of the sun. Therefore, if a new moon or a full moon takes place at such a time, the effect insofar as the shadow is concerned, is as if an object were slightly to the west of a building in the morning, and not far enough to the north or south of the east-west line passing through the center of the building but that it is completely or partially covered by the shadow of the building. The object is thus partially or totally eclipsed.

Because the moon's orbit slightly alters its inclination to the ecliptic, and because the semi-diameter of the moon changes slightly due to its varying distance from the earth, the distance the full moon or new moon must be from one of the moon's nodes to make an eclipse varies within certain limits. If the sun at new moon is within 15° 21′ of either node it must be a solar eclipse. If the sun at new moon is farther than 18° 31′ from either of the nodes it cannot be a solar eclipse. If the sun at full moon is within 9° 30′ of either node it must be a lunar eclipse. If the sun at full moon is farther than 12° 15′ from either node it cannot be a lunar eclipse. With modern ephemerides which give the zodiacal longitude of sun and moon and the north node (the south node is always in the degree and minute exactly opposite in the zodiac) it is easy to determine whether a new moon or full moon is in the region which makes an eclipse obligatory, or in the region which excludes an eclipse. But when the sun at new moon is between 15° 21′ and 18° 31′ from one of the nodes, and when the sun at full moon is between 9° 30′ and 12° 15′ from one of the nodes, the Saros can be employed as the Aztecs used it to determine if the occurrence is an eclipse; or without any reference to the nodes, the Saros can thus be used to determine if any particular new moon or full moon is an eclipse.

When an eclipse series starts—that is, eclipses which continue to repeat at intervals of 18 years, 11⅓ days—the first eclipse will occur when the sun and moon are approximately 18 to the east of one of the nodes. The central line of the moon's shadow will then pass about 2,000 miles above the north pole or below the south pole of the earth; which pole depending upon which of the nodes the sun is near. The cone of the moon's shadow will not touch the surface of the earth, but a small partial eclipse will take place near the pole, due to a small part of the penumbral shadow falling there. After the Saros period the eclipse will recur, but the partial eclipse will be a little larger. Then after some 200 years in which there have been a dozen Saros periods the true shadow cone will fall on the earth near the pole and there will be in that region a total or annular eclipse of the sun.

Following this, for some 800 years, after each Saros interval there will be a return of the total or annular eclipse, which at the rate of about 200 miles toward the other pole at each return moves over the equator and off the other pole. After the total or annular eclipse thus moves off the opposite pole from the one where it started, it appears at the pole where it leaves as a partial eclipse which at each return gets smaller. After about 200 years, or about a dozen returns of the Saros intervals, even the penumbral shadow no longer touches the polar region and the series is finished. Such a series of solar eclipses from start to finish has from 68 to 75 returns, requiring from about 1150 to 1260 years. Some 25 are only partial eclipses, but around 45 in the middle of the series are central, about 18 of them being total and about 27 annular. The number varies with different eclipse series.

Lunar eclipses repeat in practically the same way, beginning with small partial eclipses, which after 13 or 14 repetitions become total, then repeating 22 or 23 times as total, to pass out after some 13 more repetitions as partial eclipses, there being some 48 or 49 in the complete lunar series, recurring regularly once in every 223 months during an interval of 865½ years.

In case of the start of an eclipse series, in which the first small partial eclipse at one of the poles had not yet taken place, and in the case of the last small partial eclipse at one of the poles of a series which was ending, it will be apparent that using the Saros period to predict the recurrence would fail. But with these rare exceptions, which are partial eclipses so small as to have little significance, with a table of eclipses which had occurred during one Saros period, any or all of the eclipses which would occur in any other Saros period within a space of several hundred years could be readily ascertained by using the Saros interval. And by means of the Triskelion calendar, which embraced three Saros periods, the Aztecs were able to predict the return after 54 years, 33 days, of any eclipse which had been visible to them of which a record had been kept.

From a table of new moons already recorded, counting ahead from each 18 years, 11 and one-third days would give the dates on which the new moons of any given year would occur. Furthermore, by using the Triskelion Calendar, with its period of 54 years, 33 days, the position of the new moon in the sky, relative to the midheaven could also be predetermined; for after this interval it would be 13½ degrees eastward of its position on the previous occasion.

In mundane astrology it is the practice, both ancient and modern, to erect a chart for the exact time of new moon for the particular place about which information is desired, and to use this as a chart indicating the events which will happen during the following lunar month. Now by the use of the Triskelion period of three Saros the Aztecs were able to determine long years in advance, from the new moons recorded during a past Triskelion period, where either a new moon or an eclipse would occur in reference to the midheaven. And this, in turn, would give them the time of day of its occurrence. If it occurred 13½ degrees from the midheaven, for instance, this signified it occurred 54 minutes before or after noon; before noon if east of the M.C., after noon if west of the M.C.

As explained in Brotherhood of Light lessons, the aspects made by the sun and moon during the lunar month following a new moon to the places of the planets in the new moon chart, indicate both the time and the nature of the events, within a limit of 24 hours, which will transpire at the place for which the new moon chart is erected. And it is my opinion that the ancient astrologers made use of just such new moon charts, and the aspects formed by sun and moon during the month to the planets' places.

At least the Aztecs, with their Triskelion Calendar, together with their Swastika Calendar, had devised implements which were quite sufficient to determine solar eclipses, and thus when the disasters accompanying them would take place, to determine when each new moon would occur and to set a chart showing its relative distance from the M.C., and to determine the exact days in advance on which the sun and moon made every aspect formed to the places of the planets throughout the month. For, as already explained, the Swastika Calendar gave the positions of both sun and moon in the zodiac on every day.

Chapter 6

Stellar Religion of the American Indian

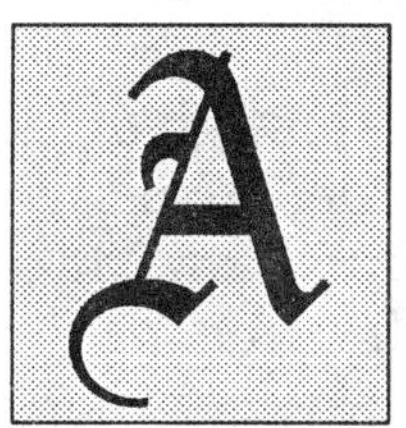s a prelude to a discussion of the stellar religion of the early inhabitants of America, mention should be made of the early appearance of man on this continent. Until 1937, the most early type was believed to have been the Folsom Man. If he arrived as early as it is held he did, it is difficult to see how, with an ice-sheet over much of America, he could have crossed the shallow strait, or possibly the low land bridge, that then connected Siberia and Alaska, to at last find his way to the grassy plains of the eastern slope of the Rockies, there to pursue vast herds of bison. It is supposed it took many generations to make the migration, but it was not until the ice-sheets melted back that forests again grew in the north, and until they did the difficulty of procuring food would make such movement hazardous. But whether he came by way of such a land bridge, or directly from Atlantis or Mu, the known facts about this Folsom Man are summed up in *The Literary Digest*, issue of August 17, 1935, thus:

> Last week, Dr. John C. Merriam, President of the Carnegie Institute of Washington, summed up the recent evidence of the antiquity of man in America:
>
> Typical stone points of the type known as Folsom have been found in a cave near Carlsbad, New Mexico, together with bones of extinct types of horse, bison, and a goat-like animal resembling the musk-ox.
>
> At Clovis, New Mexico, Folsom points were found with the remains of elephants and ground sloths. At Folsom, New Mexico at Frederick, Oklahoma, and other locations in the Great Plains, they have been found with bones of an extinct type of bison.

In Minnesota, parts of human skeletons have been found in deposits laid down in or near glacial lakes, probably as old, or nearly as old, as the last glaciation in the region—approximately 20,000 years.

None of these occurrences, admitted Dr. Merriam, indicates that man is native to America."

At the same time, the American record 'appears to extend back into a period that either is an older extension of our recent epoch, or one representing the latter portion of the Pleistocene time.' The Pleistocene was the geological epoch which included the ice age.

Ten years after the discovery of the Folsom Man, through excavations in 1937, indisputable evidence of a still older man was unearthed in the Sandia Mountains, near Albuquerque, New Mexico. Quoting from the July, 1940, issue of The Scientific American:

A cave man of ancient America gradually took form. This, in itself, is not remarkable, for evidence of a very early type of American who had hunted now extinct mammals and who lived during the rainy period just after the last glaciation have been found before. Of these, one of the most famous is the so-called Folsom Man, named from the little town of Folsom, New Mexico. Folsom Man was a hunter who ranged up and down the foothills of the Rocky Mountains hunting a peculiar type of bison or buffalo now long extinct. This type of man left traces of his passing in a distinctive type of javelin point which looks like a short bayonet with a groove running up either side. These folsom points have been found from Saskatchewan to Texas, and for the last decade have been considered as indicating the earliest known human evidence in the New World.

At first it was thought that the Sandia evidence was only another phase of the Folsom, a variation perhaps, or another tribe. Results of the latest digging, however, have given conclusive evidence of a group of men who hunted the green hills of New Mexico long before even the Folsom Man. These were contemporaries of the mammoth and the mastodon, and of the American horse and the camel and the savage predators who preyed upon them. Evidence of these earlier animals is not founded on guesswork or even on clues, but is based on the science of stratigraphy. Stratigraphic evidence is derived from the long known fact that he who is first gets in on the ground floor.

Above the layer of material in which the implements of the

Sandia Man were found is a stratum of water-deposited yellow ochre such as it is believed was deposited by the long rainy period at the end of the last glaciation. Above this yellow ochre stratum in the same cave were found evidence that after the rainy period following the retreat of the last ice sheet the cave had dried out and had been used over a long period by the Folsom Man. Still above this Folsom deposit was a crust which had sealed in all below it. Thus the stratigraphic positions of the artifacts of the Sandia Man are considered by archaeologists to constitute proof that he lived in America before the end of the ice age, that is, in the Pleistocene epoch.

We do not expect nomadic tribes which live by hunting either to develop a high degree of culture or to preserve in detail any complex system of knowledge. Their time and energy are too largely expended in following the game they hunt. Culture thrives only where there is considerable leisure and a fixed abode. These are made possible only through agriculture, which yields a food supply for a settled habitation. And in ancient America agriculture was chiefly practiced in the south.

Now if we are to judge from both the three-armed swastika, or Triskelion, and the four-armed swastika, such as those at the right and left of the lower central figure in the illustration on page 4—which are common forms unearthed in Europe and Asia as well as in America—the essential factors of the stellar religion were once known and observed on various continents. And the inference is that, in each of widely separated areas, it was derived from a single still more ancient source; that it was, in fact, the religion of the more enlightened races of lands now submerged beneath the waters of the Atlantic and Pacific.

As a naturalist, and a student of the development and dispersal of new life forms on the earth, I find no evidence on which to base the popular conception that the inhabitants of these ancient lands were skilled in the construction or use of machinery. Nor do I believe they were the equal of present-day astronomers in making precise calculations.

They knew vastly more about the unseen world, about spiritual laws, and about the influence of astrological energies upon human life, than does the average scientist, because they had specialized in such research for innumerable generations. And they had been helped in their studies, as we often are helped, by those who no longer reside on the earth, but still continue their studies. The present-day scientist knows nothing about these things because his prejudices, biased by orthodox religion even though he is a materialist, lead him to ignore them. We moderns owe a great debt to those who labored in the ancient past. But it is unnecessary to glorify them in achievements of which they felt no need and which they did not contemplate.

That which was their chief interest was human life and its possibilities, both here and hereafter. Not being restricted by narrow orthodox tradition, they were willing to believe the irrefutable evidence of experience that planetary energies have an influence over human life and destiny. And they studied this influence, not in the sense of helpless fatality, but for the same purpose moderns study the weather; to be able to take advantage of it. Yet if they were to classify such invisible influences, and thus be able to take advantage of those which were favorable, and to escape the destructive power of those inimical, they must possess themselves of some means of locating their positions in the sky on any given date. And it is to their everlasting credit, not possessing intricate mathematical apparatus, that they devised and used a method which was adequate to meet practical astrological requirements.

The Moundbuilders

The large central part of the illustration on page 4 is such a device. It is a boulder, 15 inches long, 12 inches wide, and 3 inches thick. The middle of the stone bears a highly polished disc, representing the sun, in the middle of which—as we now represent the sun's symbol—a small hole is etched. The stone, photographs of which have been sent to the principal museums of the world, was presented to Colonel Fordyce. It was found a few years ago by a boat builder on the bank of Lake Hamilton, which is formed by damming the water of the Ouachita River near Hot Springs, Arkansas. Below the stone on the same page is pictured, between the four-armed swastika and the three-armed swastika, a date stone found on an ancient tomb in Tennessee.

Even as in Europe and provincial America, where a churchyard was the choice of burial spots, the temples of the pre-Columbian Americans were commonly associated with the bones of the dead. Several thousand large mounds, and uncounted smaller ones, all manmade, are scattered over two-thirds of the states. They rise above the plains from the Great Lakes to Louisiana, and from Georgia to Florida. From Florida they extend both west to Texas and north to the state of New York.

As we here are concerned with the religion of these people there will be no discussion of the copper breastplates and copper hatchets and magic ornaments, except to mention, in connection with the latter, that the evidence is conclusive that the builders of these earthworks believed in the efficacy of the power of thought. Implements and food buried with the dead reveal their conviction of the survival of the personality, and there is abundant evidence that they practiced spirit communion.

Two of these mounds, both of which are in Ohio, are in the form of a serpent. The one in Adams County winds along the edge of a cliff beside a river to the length of 1,254 feet. In front of its mouth is an oval mound, like an egg which it is about to swallow. This, of course, portrays the same conception as that of the Hopi Indian when in his dance he carries a snake in his mouth, as will be explained shortly. It relates to the eclipse period of the Triskelion Calendar, the tradition being—still expressed in the common name of the moon's nodes—that when an eclipse takes place the sun is being devoured by a dragon.

In addition to the more common hill-like mounds in Ohio and Wisconsin, there are embankment mounds representing squares, circles, and other geometric figures. Mr. Henry Lee Stoddard has given these earthworks careful study. In his book, *When It Was Light*, he points out, giving numerous calculations and diagrams by way of explanation, that they were built after the same astronomical ratios employed in the construction of the Pyramid of Gizah in Egypt. Since Mr. Stoddard's book appeared, steam shovel cuts through some of the hill-like mounds have revealed that the larger of these actually have within them a pyramidal structure. Excavation shows that these mounds were started as small burial heaps. Then they were built into the form of a tall pointed pyramid. Only later were they covered with soil, and finally with a fine coat of gravel, into the form of a rounded hill.

On the summit of some of these mounds, high and flat-topped, were temples. Both the Mayas and the Aztecs used the flat tops of their pyramids as stellar observatories and for religious purposes. The largest of the Indian mounds is the Cahoka mound near East St. Louis, Illinois. It covers 16 acres and is 104 feet high.

Instead of making surmise regarding the rituals of stellar import conducted on these mounds, or of further indicating their significance as places where the living communed with the dead, the evidence will be more positive if we examine the Arkansas Astrological Stone and the Date Stone from the Tennessee tomb. Neither the Date Stone from the Tennessee tomb, which is reproduced at the center bottom of the illustration on page 4, nor the Arkansas Astrological Stone which forms the main picture on page 4, can be comprehended apart from some knowledge of the Triskelion and Swastika calendars explained in Chapter Five. These, at one time, were probably used in many parts of the world, as well as by the Aztecs.

The Aztec Triskelion Calendar, reproduction of which after Clavigero is pictured at the upper right-hand corner of the illustration on page 4, enabled those familiar with its use, as I explained in Chapter 5, to determine any distance in the future or in the past when an eclipse would occur and where it would be visible; also when New Moons would occur, and which house of a birthchart they would occupy. This Triskelion Calendar, together with the Swastika Calendar, was sufficient to enable those familiar with them to set a New Moon chart and to determine the exact days on which the Sun and Moon made every aspect to the planets throughout the month; for the Swastika Calendar gave the position of both Sun and Moon in the zodiac for every day. Not only so, but these positions of the Sun and Moon could thus be determined ten, twenty, fifty, or any number of years in advance.

I wonder how many modern astrological students can ascertain the zodiacal positions of the Sun and Moon, and their house positions, just fifty years from the time they read this!

By the Swastika System there are four equal seasons embracing 364 days. As the year employed had 365¼ days, to account for this discrepancy each year had at its end a festival day, and each fourth year contained two festival days, by The Aztecs called "enmontemi" or useless days, because on these days no work was done.

The year commenced at the winter solstice, about December 22, and each of the four seasons following contained exactly 91 days, composed of 7 weeks of 13 days each. The name of each of the four seasons and the name of each of the 13 days are given in

Chapter 5, where also will be found a picture of the famous Aztec Calendar Stone together with a more detailed picture of the single season scheme as preserved by Veytia. Like the Arkansas Astrological Stone, the Aztec Calendar Stone covers but one season. Around this Aztec stone there are 20 pictographs. Thirteen of them are the names of the days of the week, as are those immediately around the circumference of the Sun in the Arkansas Stone. The other 7 are the names of the weeks in a season.

Let us compare the names of the weeks used by the Aztecs with those used by the people who employed the Arkansas Stone. The pictures thus designating the weeks on the Aztec Stone follow each other thus: 1. Jaguar. 2. Eagle. 3. Bird. 4. Sun. 5. Flint. 6. Rain. 7. Flower. On the Arkansas Stone pictured on page 4, starting to the left of the top after the Aztec precedent they run thus: 1. Turtle. 2. Bear. 3. Fish Duck. 4. Alligator. 5. Antelope. 6. Fish. 7. Whale. On the Arkansas Astrological Stone, in addition, just above the whale there is a phallic emblem which is being energized by the lightning which descends from a scorpion.

As presently to be explained, the Hopi Indians of today believe the creative function only manifests through the sex-influence of the zodiacal sign Scorpio, which in its higher function they picture as an eagle, or Thunderbird, and in its destructive action by the lightning.

Among the people who used this Arkansas Astrological Stone, the scorpion is used to depict the constellation in the manner most familiar to us. And as this desert denizen depicts the destructive action of sex, the lightning to them probably indicated all the creative energy ruled over by the eighth zodiacal sign. At least, the lightning coming down from the stellar Scorpion to the lingham below, with a germ already developed, as they had seen it develop when beans or corn were placed in the warm moist earth, indicates that they exalted sex to a position of unusual importance. It suggests that—as did the Ancient Masons, as explained in detail in Brotherhood of Light Course IV, *Ancient Masonry*—they believed the creative energy could be employed not merely for grosser ends, but also to raise their vibratory rates to more spiritual planes of endeavor.

Between the phallic symbol and the disc of the Sun in the center of the stone are five portrayals of the Moon. These are not those of the modern almanac, but represent the actual appearance of the Moon when it makes aspects to the Sun as follows, reading from left to right: First sextile after New Moon, First square after New Moon, opposition aspect or Full Moon, Last square before New Moon, Last sextile before New Moon.

We have no way of ascertaining whether the astrology practiced by the Americans who designed this stone was a crude, clumsy approximate science, or if it can be compared favorably in its precision with our own. We do know, however, that they recognized the major aspects of the Moon to the Sun, as these are pictured. And we know that they were able to ascertain in advance the aspects of the Moon to the Sun, and the house position of each, as the Arkansas Stone was designed for that purpose.

Both Mayas and Aztecs, who used similar devices, were familiar with the planets also, and used them in their astrological practice. We may infer with some assurance, therefore, that this people also recognized the planets and had a knowledge of the quality of energy radiated by each.

I believe there has now been set forth conclusive evidence in reference to the Stellar Religion of the Mound Builders that they:

1. Believed in the power of thought to alter circumstances (directed thinking).

2. Paid homage to the spiritualizing influence of love (induced emotion).

3. Were aware of the after-life through mediumship or other forms of ESP, probably both, and held communion with those who had passed to the after-life.

4. Recognized that the heavenly bodies exercise an influence over human life and destiny (astrology).

The Pueblo Dwellers

In Egypt, Assyria, Peru, Mexico and Brittany there are numerous menhirs; single stones placed upright. They were erected as symbols of the sun, vertical positions symbolizing the direction from which the sun's hottest rays fall upon the earth. An elaboration of the simple menhir is the round tower. Such towers are found throughout the world, and everywhere are similar in character and construction, usually being built with but a single entrance some distance above the ground. There are some one hundred and fifty of these round towers in Ireland, running from eight to fifteen feet in diameter and from seventy to one hundred thirty feet high, with an opening around twenty feet from the ground.

A similar round tower, so ancient that science can but speculate as to the period when it was built, is located in Rhode Island, another in the Marcos Valley in Colorado, and still a third in Yucatan. Some of these stone towers are to be found in England, one on the Isle of Man, three in Scotland, and others in Corsica. They are found throughout the East, and it is said that the famous Leaning Tower of Pisa, Italy, is of the same construction as the round towers of India, Arabia and Sicily.

These round towers generally were circular in form and in their general construction elaborated the creative symbolism of the sun. In addition they were also often observatories. From the bottom of such a tower stars on the zenith may be seen in daylight. Those built in pre-Columbus days in Southwest United States were dubbed Indian Watchtowers. An exact and impressive reproduction of one of these ancient so-called watchtowers has been built with the labor of Hopi Indians on the edge of the Grand Canyon of Arizona.

Adjacent to the temple observatories now called watchtowers were the Kivas, which were underground ceremonial chambers where Indian initiates could go to converse with their departed friends or commune with the Great Spirit. On the walls of the watchtowers were strangely beautiful symbols associated with the Stellar Religion of these Indians. Even as Akhenaten developed a beautiful and distinctive Stellar Art in Egypt, so did the Southwest Indians in connection with their religion develop a beautiful Stellar Art of their own. Both were developed about the ideas inherited from the colonists of Atlantis and Mu, and each according to its own technique was associated with healing. The method of Akhenaten is indicated in Chapter 1. And here it should be mentioned that the Sand Paintings of the American Indians were an essential part of the technique by which they tuned in on, and directed to the accomplishment of a definite purpose, such as healing, planetary and other invisible energies.

Stellar Art, as painted on the walls of temples and tombs, may yet be seen in Egypt after a lapse of 3,300 years. And while reproductions would be necessary to give an idea of the beauty of the Stellar Art of the Southwest Indians, it may be said also that the wonders performed by the initiates of the sand paintings were the equal of any produced in India.

These American initiates, few of whom are now left, however, considered occult powers sacred. They never brought them into play to satisfy curiosity, or merely to create wonder; but only to heal the sick, to cause rain for the crops, or to bring about some other condition of benefit to their people.

Even as in ancient Egypt, initiation and secret ceremonies were conducted underground. These underground chambers, as already mentioned, were called kivas. Only initiates were admitted to the kivas, or took part in the ceremonies conducted there, and they guarded their knowledge jealously.

Through the sensational columns of the Sunday supplements most people know of the snake dance, in which live snakes are handled. But this is only the short public part of a long ritual, mostly carried out in the underground kiva by initiates. Among the other ceremonies held in the kiva is one at the winter solstice, one at the vernal equinox, and one at the summer solstice. The initiates, even among present-day Indians, possess sufficient astrological knowledge to be able to determine these dates. Should you wish a detailed account of these ceremonies, it is to be found in *The Annual Report of the Smithsonian Institute* for the year 1918, in an article on Sun Worship of the Hopi Indians, by J. Walter Fewkes, Chief, Bureau of American Ethnology.

But before describing either the Hopi snake dance ceremony or their rite of "Calling back the Sun," as both the influence of the Planet Pluto and the significance of the Moon's Nodes are included as important elements of these ceremonies, to make them understandable we should first discuss these two astrological factors. As to Pluto, let me call attention to the four things which Greek mythology asserts about him:

1. He was the god of the underworld, that is, of the after-life. This conforms to the rulership of the eighth house of a birthchart and to the zodiacal sign Scorpio.

2. He was a kidnapper. He kidnapped Persephone, the daughter of Demeter, goddess of the harvest, and took her to the underworld to be his bride. And in our mundane and natal astrological research we find kidnapping, whenever present, to be coincident with outstanding influences from the planet Pluto.

3. Pluto has a violently destructive side; for after the kidnap-

ping of Persephone the earth no longer yielded its harvest. There was then a depression; even as the greatest financial depression known, and widespread droughts which made a "dust-bowl" of previously fertile regions in the U.S., were coincident with the discovery of the planet Pluto.

4. Pluto has a spiritual and constructive side. He was persuaded to restore Persephone to her mother for two-thirds of the year, and as a result there were again abundant harvests.

All our research concerning this inner plane planet tends to strengthen the conviction that Pluto has two opposite natures, and that he is coruler of Scorpio. Demeter, goddess of the fruitful soil and agriculture, is one aspect of the Moon. The kidnaping of her daughter, the capturing of the Moon's own flesh and blood, seems to fit well with the present conception of astrologers that Pluto, while also possessing the drastic force of Mars, is the upper octave of the moon.

Scorpio, with Mars as its ruler, is never milk-and-water. It is either the Scorpion of the desert, the female of which, as soon as her lust is gratified, devours her mate. Or it is the Eagle, soaring on the wings of spirit, even into the face of the sun.

Now anyone who has visited an Indian curio store, or who has dropped off the train for a few minutes at Albuquerque or Gallup, New Mexico, will have been struck by the fact that the two popular emblems of Indian jewelry are the Swastika and the Thunderbird.

The Swastika is an Aztec calendar by which, as previously explained, on any day of the year the relation of the moon to the sun can be determined. It also indicates in an unmistakable manner the derivation of our modern playing cards. Each of the four arms contains compartments numbered from 1 to 13, bearing, like a suit of playing cards, the emblem of one season. And there is a 53rd emblem in the center, corresponding to the joker.

The creative function of sun and moon, according to the Indians, can only manifest through sex, the zodiacal sign Scorpio which they pictured as an Eagle, or Thunderbird. And instead of using the scorpion to picture the destructive side of sex, or Pluto, they used an even more expressive universal symbol, the lightning bolt. Lightning, although now developed in atom smashing laboratories, has not yet been harnessed. We have witnessed lightning at no constructive work. But we have seen trees or houses which have been destroyed by it. And because of these associations it becomes a fitting symbol of a violently destructive force; and has so been used on the 16th Major Arcanum of the Egyptian Tarot.

In 1933, when the first political administration of the U.S. following the discovery of Pluto went into office, there was passed a National Recovery Act which theoretically embraced both sides of Pluto. It asked for cooperation for the common good—Upper Pluto—to limit hours and increase wages and thus restrict production. It also gave to the Administration coercive powers which, as well as the curtailment of production of things wanted by people, is typically a Lower-Pluto expression. This NRA adopted as its symbol the Blue Eagle, cards on which the eagle was pictured being displayed in the shop windows and homes of those observing the NRA code. This Blue Eagle was none other than the Indian Thunderbird, their symbol of Pluto, holding in its left, or adverse foot, the lightning of destruction. In its right, or constructive foot, it held the cogwheel, a universal symbol of construction through cooperation. Thus it symbolized that unless cooperative effort were made, violent destruction would follow.

The Indians were unfamiliar with the cogwheel. But they knew about the beneficence of the planet Jupiter, and had a gem ruled by the sign Sagittarius, on which they greatly relied to attract the Jupiterian power. Therefore, as witnessed in all their better Thunderbird jewelry, to call out only the constructive side of Pluto, they placed within the bird's breast a setting of blue turquoise, and made of him a Blue Eagle.

The Dragon In the Sky
While it is a common thing to note the position of the Moon's Nodes in a birthchart, the symbol used, and what it represents, and why it always moves backward through the zodiac, are most mysterious to many astrological students. The points where the orbital paths of two heavenly bodies intersect are called their Nodes. As none of the other planets moves in the same plane as the orbit of the earth, each of their orbits must cut the orbit of the earth at two points. Therefore, not only the moon, but each of the planets also, has both an Ascending Node and a Descending Node. That is, each of these orbital paths is in the plane which cuts

the plane of the earth's orbit at an angle. The plane of the moon's orbit inclines thus to the plane of the earth's orbit at an angle of a little over five degrees.

When the moon or a planet is close to its nodes, there commonly is a right-angled gravitational pull which tends temporarily to increase the inclination of the plane of its orbit to that of the earth. In the case of the moon, except twice a year when the sun is at the moon's nodes, and twice a month when the moon is square to the sun, its crossing a node is thus influenced by a right-angled pull.

After it moves away from the earth's orbit the right-angled pull diminishes and it again assumes the same inclination it previously had. But the new plane of its orbit, and consequently the nodes where the orbits intersect, have shifted back due to the mentioned right-angled pull. Thus the moon's nodes move in a continuous retrograde manner around the zodiac. In a somewhat similar manner the nodes of all the planets, without exception, retrograde through the zodiac. But the Ascending Node of the moon, where it crosses the path of the sun in coming north, is the only one given in the common ephemeris. Because the moon's nodes do thus retrograde through the zodiac, the time for the sun to pass around from a node to the same node again is less than a year. It is 346.62 days; a period which, as eclipses are dependent upon the sun's proximity to a node, as explained in Chapter Five, is called an "eclipse year." The nodes thus move westward completely around the zodiac in about 19 years.

These nodes are written by using a conventional serpent. If the arch of the serpent's back is up—as it is shown in the common ephemeris—it is called the Dragon's Head, and signifies the ascending node. If the arch of the serpent's back is down, it is called the Dragon's Tail, and indicates the descending node. Thus are they associated with the dragon, still pictured in the sky as the constellation Draco, because when an eclipse takes place the sun or moon symbolically is then devoured by a dragon or, in the case of a partial eclipse is gnawed upon; a symbolism that is taken literally by the more ignorant Eastern peoples.

An eclipse of the sun, which can take place only when the sun is close to the Dragon's Head or Dragon's Tail, indicates that disaster will befall some section of the region touched by the eclipse shadow. It is, consequently, regarded with terror by primitive people with inherited stellar traditions. It was probably the observation that calamities were coincident with, or shortly followed, solar eclipses in the region touched by the shadow that led many ancient people to associate the dragon with the source of evil. Such clearly seems to be the import of Revelation, Chap. 20:

> And I saw an angel come down from heaven, and having the key of the bottomless pit and a great chain in his hand. And he laid hold on the dragon, and that old serpent, which is the Devil, and Satan, and bound him a thousand years. And cast him into the bottomless pit, and shut him up, and set a seal upon him, that he should deceive the nations no more, till the thousand years be fulfilled: and after that he must be loosed a little season.

The legends of India relate that Krishna met and slew this noisome dragon, whose poisonous breath withered the crops, bred famine, and whose movement through the countryside left death and destruction in its wake. In legendary Christendom it was St. George who played the valiant hero, and after a long and violent battle succeeded in leaping on the back of the scaly monster and driving his great two-handed sword straight through its wicked heart.

But it is in China that more attention is paid to the malefic dragon than elsewhere. There the populace habitually spends far more energy in ceremonies to prevent misfortune than in observances to attract the good. And the most drastic of such observances is the pageant each year, which is described in Brotherhood of Light lesson No. 78, in which the dragon is met and after great struggle vanquished.

The Hopi Snake Dance

The Hopi snake dance always commences when the sun is in the Sagittarius decanate of the sun's sign Leo. There are four snake hunts, commencing at sunrise of four consecutive days; one to the north, one to the west, one to the south and one to the east. These represent the four seasons represented by the four arms of the swastika and the four suits of our playing cards. The active days of the ceremony are just 13, the number of cards in each suit and the number of compartments in each swastika arm.

In the public part of the snake dance also, even as our face cards are grouped as King, Queen and Jack of each suit, so the initiates always come forward and dance in groups of three. Furthermore, as the swastika is a Solar-Lunar calendar, so this is a Solar-Lunar dance. But it embraces more than the swastika, as it also relates to the triskelion calendar of three arms instead of four, by which eclipses were predicted.

The "carrier" in the dance represents the King of face cards and the sun in the sky. He carries the snake in his mouth because of the ancient tradition that when an eclipse takes place the sun is being devoured by a dragon. The snake in his mouth is the original design of the dragon's head and dragon's tail of astrology, where alone eclipses take place. It also is the original symbol used for the sign Leo.

The snake, from its phallic significance, was sacred to the sun and was the emblem of masculine creative energy on every plane of endeavor. Thus, to indicate enlightenment the Egyptians pictured the serpent at the brow of their greatest characters. But Typhon, who created only evil, was pictured with the serpent emerging from his belly.

Accompanying the "carrier" in the dance is his consort, corresponding to the Queen of face cards and the moon in the sky. His left hand throughout the dance remains on the left shoulder of the "carrier," and still further to indicate his feminine attributes he soothes and pacifies with a feather the snake carried in the mouth of his dancing partner. He is called the "hugger."

The third member of the dancing trio, called the "gatherer," looks after the snakes as they are dropped to see that none are stepped on. But here, instead of being concerned with him, we are interested in the circumstance that the snake dance ritual—through which the Indians contact their friends on the inner plane, and procure help, among other things, in warding off drought which frequently accompanies an eclipse of the sun where visible—always ends after the sun has passed into the first, or harvest, decanate of the harvest sign Virgo.

Hopi Indian girls, from puberty until marriage, wear their hair in a carefully prepared representation of the squash blossom. But the Virgin Mother pictured in the sky is represented among our face cards by the Queen of Spades who bears, not merely the blossom of virginity in her hand, as do the other queens, but also the flaming torch which indicates the virgin conception.

The Egyptians in their pageants to the Motherhood of Isis

carried a musical instrument called the sistrum, which they jingled. It was a thin metal frame in the form of the uterus, through which rods were passed to represent the Solar-Lunar forces in union. And it was keyed, according to tradition, to the creative vibratory rate of Nature which, according to their ideas, procured not merely the material harvest, but mental genius and spiritual immortality as well.

The Indians did not have horses until the Spaniards brought them to America, and thus indicated the Sagittarius decanate of Leo not by the Centaur, but by their fleetest four-footed animal, the antelope. And during the public part of the snake dance antelope initiates on the sidelines shake white gourds filled with seeds, not tuned to any particular key, but identical in shape and symbolism with the Egyptian sistrum.

Now the snake, representing the fifth house influence of Leo, indicated creative energy, which was given its particular constructive or destructive trend only through its association with Pluto, their Thunderbird, the ruler of Scorpio. Both the deadly rattlesnake and the lightning painted on the bodies of the antelope initiates were meant to indicate the violence of its destructive trends. The Egyptians, to express this, commonly used the T with the point down, and this is one significance of the 22nd Major Arcanum of their tarot. Birds, because they fly above the sordid earth, were symbols of higher influences, and their feathers represented spiritual trends. Thus we perceive that the feather used in the snake dance to soothe the snakes and render them harmless was the emblem of the spiritualizing influence of woman over man. And this indicates the true significance of the feathered serpent, which was used by the Indians and was of paramount importance to the religion of the Mayas. The feathers on the serpent revealed that the creative energy was directed to constructive and spiritual ends.

To contact a spiritual plane the mind must be held on a spiritual vibratory level, and this can be done by acquiring and maintaining an appropriate emotion or mood. Such an emotion or mood is felt only when the thought or environmental stimulation produces a definite electrical condition in some portion of the nervous system. An individual may think a thing in a coldly intellectual manner without much feeling. In that case the electrical energies generated by the thought mostly are used up in imparting vibrations to the brain cells. On the other hand, the same individual may think of some emergency situation and immediately feel a profound shock over his whole body. The nervous excitement, which means the intensity of the electrical currents flowing over his nerves, may be so great that his knees knock together, his teeth chatter, and his hands shake in spite of all his efforts to appear unconcerned.

If the nervous system does not generate powerful electrical energies, no matter what image is in his mind, he does not feel strongly. But those who used the feathered serpent, or a feather to soothe a serpent in their ceremonies, believed that the creative energies of Pluto could be used both to induce a spiritual mood, and to generate the electrical energy to sustain it.

Calling Back the Sun

At the winter solstice, three days before Christmas, the sun passes from Sagittarius, the Archer, to its lowest position in the tomb of winter, at the commencement of Capricorn. The nights are longest then, and the earth is captive, bound by frost in the hands of the evil forces of the underworld, where she can bring forth no fruit. To indicate this the Hopi Indians kidnap, after the manner of Pluto in Greek mythology, a maiden and take her beneath the earth where initiates are assembled in the kiva.

She is seated back of a mound of earth to the right of an altar erected to the feathered serpent. Near the mound are some arrows. The front of the altar has a disc-like aperture through which the effigy of a feathered serpent sticks its head and moves about. The sun is always represented in association with this altar, and at the village of Orabi is painted on a movable screen.

Even as we at Christmas adorn a tree with presents to indicate the fruits of the branch held in the hand of Hercules, picturing the middle decanate of the harvest sign Virgo, in anticipation of the harvest which will follow this turning back of the sun, so before the feathered serpent altar are ears of corn and seeds of such other things as the Indian hopes to harvest.

The pipe is smoked, which signifies to the Indians who pass it from one to another, that all are of one mind, that is, in rapport, and seek guidance from the spirit world. Ceremonially smoking the pipe is their ritual of "Peace on Earth, Good Will to Men."

One of the initiates then starts blowing on a bone whistle, in imitation of an eagle's scream, and immediately on the roof of the kiva overhead something starts tramping about, and shortly, even as Santa Claus comes down the chimney, so an Indian dressed like a Thunderbird throws down a ball of sacred meal and descends the ladder. He sits in front of the kidnapped maiden for a time, then leaps to his feet with a cry, grabs up the arrows and throws them into the mound of earth. These arrows, symbol of the zodiacal sign from which the sun is passing, represent the beneficent influence of its ruler, Jupiter. Speeches, addressed to the feathered serpent also indicate that the constructive side of Pluto, the Thunderbird, is being brought into action. The ball of sacred meal which he threw down the hatch into the kiva indicates his willingness to help procure a harvest.

The turning back of the sun, and its correspondence in the electromagnetic energies of man, are pictured by the emblem held in the hand of the Jack of Spades, which is the card of Capricorn. The victory, however, is not granted without a struggle, and the initiates, as in the Degree of the Cross of Ancient Masonry, divide into two contending ranks and stage a mock fight, to indicate the struggle between the forces of Light and the forces of the Shadow. But after a time the Brethren of the Light gain supremacy. The violent and destructive side of Pluto has been overcome, and its constructive powers have been utilized to free the kidnapped maiden, and to restore fertility to the mound which symbolizes the earth.

The harvest gained by those who espouse the cause of the feathered serpent as against the lightning, however, is not merely of this plane. To those who adopt the religion of the constructive side of Pluto—as signified by the religious sign Sagittarius, in the use of the arrows by the Thunderbird—physical existence becomes impregnated with the determination TO CONTRIBUTE THEIR UTMOST TO UNIVERSAL WELFARE, and this makes certain, both here and hereafter, a bounteous spiritual harvest.

Chapter 7

Astrological Significance of Holidays

he operation of spiritual laws often best can be illustrated by their parallel effects on the affairs of earth. The Law of Correspondences is such a law. In effect, the principle involved—which has ramifications as broad as the universe itself—is that bodies and minds move more easily by flowing along in the same direction as a stream of force than across the current or against it. In the low-velocity physical world this is easy to picture, as we all have had ample experience with currents of water and currents of air, and have felt the impulse to go along with them, and the resistance they offered when we tried to move in some other direction.

But because so few of us have consciously had ample experiences of the high-velocity inner plane type, it is very difficult to picture how inner plane currents exert a pressure that is similar, except that additional properties are involved. Yet while such pressures, which lie at the base of the law of correspondences, are difficult to reconstruct in the imagination, they are exceedingly simple to point out in example. When, for instance, a child is born, he enters physical life at the moment the signs and planets rather closely map the thought organization of his astral body; when the regions thus mapped permit the stream of high-velocity planetary energy to flow freely through them. It is the application of the principle of least resistance. It is easier for the child to be born then than at a time when astral currents are flowing against his birth.

Furthermore, if the divergence between the organization of his astral body and the planetary currents mapped by his birthchart is too great, the child does not live. Too much astral pressure against him will stop his life. And in a similar way, a question to be answered by Horary Astrology is asked when the planets map the conditions relating to it rather than at some other time, because to ask it at some other time would mean too great a mental effort bucking astral headwinds.

As I said, this principle is as wide as the universe in its ramifications. But to illustrate one phase of its application, it is instructive to list the various persistent holidays, and show its invariable operation where they are concerned. For, just as a child born when the astrological correspondences do not coincide with its character does not live, so also a holiday, or recurrent festival, if established at a time when the astrological positions do not correspond, falls immediately into disuse.

The sun is the source of that vitality which gives length of life, and its position in the zodiac during its annual journey around it is the index by which people chiefly determine the time for observing holidays. I mean that we time Christmas, New Year's Day, Fourth of July, etc., by the day of the month, which in turn is determined by the station of the sun in the zodiac. Therefore, in seeking the correspondences which determine whether or not a holiday or festival once born will live, and continue to be observed, we chiefly look to the zodiacal position of the sun.

This path of the sun, called the zodiac, was carefully studied by the Wise Men of the East, and mapped into divisions, each of which was discerned to have a special influence. They divided this apparent path of the sun into 12 major divisions of equal extent, called signs of the zodiac. Then, because they found they exerted each a distinct influence, they divided each sign into three equal subdivisions of 10 degrees, called decanates. Through long ages of painstaking observation they ascertained the precise influence upon human life and the spiritual significance of the 12 zodiacal signs and 36 decanates. Then, by means of symbolic pictographs, they portrayed this influence and spiritual significance by designs traced among the stars.

In discerning the nature of astral currents which influence the life and nature of holidays, therefore, we have two main factors: the general rulership of the section of the zodiac occupied by the sun on the day in question, and the constellated picture which gives more detail and in addition reveals its spiritual significance. Let us, therefore, now commence with the first of the Civil Year—

New Year's Day—and follow the sun around the zodiac mentioning each in its turn, and explaining the correspondence of all the more commonly accepted holidays:

New Year's Day

In the birth of a child or in the birth of a new year, which is pictured to us even in modern times in the form of a new born babe, it is recognized that there is a mother (moon) as well as a father (sun). Therefore, whether we consider the astronomical year, which is related to the sun crossing the vernal equinox, or the civil year, which is related to the more easily determined winter solstice, the celebration is not on the day when the sun crosses the equinox or solstice, but on a subsequent day when symbolically the moon, which rules periods of gestation, has some unusual significance.

The exaltation of the moon, where it exerts its finest power, is in the sign Taurus. When the sun gets into Taurus, therefore, the mother principle has its best influence over the father. And the same idea is represented when the sun enters any Taurus decanate of the zodiac. When in winter the sun crosses the solstice from Sagittarius into Capricorn, the days are shortest and the nights longest. From that point on the days, the light—and symbolically the spiritual power—must increase. But in this journey from Matter back to Spirit, the father needs the help and cooperation of the mother; the Sun needs the assistance of the Moon. Hence the festival, and the commencement of the civil year, must embrace this factor. On New Year's Day the sun must be in the decanate of Capricorn where the moon has special significance, which is the Taurus decanate.

Epiphany

The birth of the sun, symbol of the savior of the world, as distinct from the commencement of the year, is observed on Christmas. The new life thus given to the world—for the sun rules life and vitality—must be imparted to all 12 houses of the horoscope if it is to confer its saving grace. The twelve disciples represented these twelve compartments of the astral body, each of which contains the thought cells relating to one essential department of life. Epiphany means appearance. And this appearance of the saving sun, after having revitalized all 12 houses of the horoscope, does not occur immediately after the sun is born but 12 days after Christmas, one day being used to symbolize each of the 12 houses of life.

Ground Hog Day

Uranus is the planet ruling astrology, and its sign, Aquarius, is pictured as a man measuring the influence of the stars and pouring this information from an urn down upon the children of the earth. Prognostication, therefore, is associated with Aquarius. But as giving access likewise to inner plane information, the Gemini decanate, which is occupied by the sun on February 2, has special significance. It is pictured among the constellations by a flying horse, Pegasus. Poets and those otherwise inspired, must drink from the fountain of Hippocrene, which flowed sparkling clear from Mount Helicon as the result of a blow from this horse's hoof.

In other words, the second decanate of Aquarius, the keyword of which is Inspiration, confers not merely astrological ability, but inspirational power to give it correct interpretation. And to the ground hog on February 2 is attributed such ability. He is said to come out of his hole and make an astrological observation. If the sun can be clearly seen—that is, if he sees his shadow—he concludes there will be six weeks more of winter weather. But if the sun is not visible, and his shadow cannot be seen, he decides winter is about over, and the period of hibernation can safely end.

Lincoln's Birthday

Lincoln gained lasting fame as a humanitarian. And on February 12 the sun is in the humanitarian sign, Aquarius, pictured by the Man of the sky pouring not merely knowledge, but sympathy and his blessings, from an urn upon the earth. The sun is in the last decanate of the sign, pictured by Cetus, the Whale Monster. This monster devoured the fairest youths of Greece, and Andromeda was chained to a rock for this vile creature to destroy, until she was rescued by Perseus. The keyword of the decanate is Repression.

Incidentally, Charles Darwin had voiced his abhorrence of slavery some time before Lincoln expressed an opinion about it. Like Lincoln, he was well over 6 feet tall, and was always kind and sympathetic, even writing in his youth that he sought beetles already dead for his collection, as he felt it wrong to kill them. Both men were emancipators, for what Lincoln accomplished in the abolition of bodily slavery, Darwin accomplished in the abolition of mental slavery to tyrannical tradition. These forms of human bondage are probably coevil. They had, at least, flourished since before the time of recorded history. And both were given the death blow at practically the same time, by men who both were born February 12, 1809.

Both men lived lives that in loftiness of ideals and moral integrity set them apart from others. Each accomplished a self-appointed task that contributed vastly to the welfare of all people. Neither is revered for military exploits nor for cunning. Each is honored for destroying the monster of slavery. Even as Perseus slew the hideous creature and released Andromeda, so Darwin slew the tyranny of orthodox belief and Lincoln slew the greedy institution of bodily slavery. Darwin loosed the shackles of one type of repression, and Lincoln, whose birthday is honored in the land of his birth, loosed them from another.

Valentine's Day

On February 14, which is Valentine's Day, the sun is still in the Repression decanate of Aquarius, pictured by the Whale Monster. From this danger, Andromeda was rescued by the love of her Prince Charming, Perseus, who set her free and gained her hand in marriage. The word 'valentine' is from the Norman *galantin*, meaning 'lover'; and this is the Libra decanate of the sign—that is, the marriage decanate. Therefore, especially in view of the perils pictured by the constellation Cetus, what could be more appropriate than missives of love and proposals of marriage? Efforts of true love to loose the bonds of loneliness and slay the monster of possible repression are shown.

Washington's Birthday

George Washington was the founder of a nation and its first ruler. That he demonstrated great wisdom and unselfishness to establish it as he did makes of him a great character. His birthday is observed on February 22, at a time when the sun has entered the first decanate of the sign Pisces. Pisces is a sign of restriction, and it was these restrictions which Washington removed. The decanate is pictured by Cepheus, the King; and Washington became the ruler of a newly independent country. The keyword of the decanate is Verity, and tradition relating to the famed cherry tree holds that even as a boy the founder of our country could not tell a lie. The decanate expresses the time worn thought that "The Truth

Shall Set You Free." Washington had a controversy with a king; and the type of rulership he established after that falling out set a precedent, which most of the Western World followed by adopting the republican form of government.

The Lamb and the Lion

It is said that if March comes in like a lion it goes out like a lamb, and if it comes in like a lamb it goes out like a lion. At the vernal equinox, about the 21st of March, the sun enters the sign of the Ram, which, until the sun moves far enough in it for more maturity, is commonly called a lamb. Among the Jews and many Eastern peoples, this marks the commencement, or birth, of a new year. The first decanate of the Ram is its own decanate, the young Ram, or Lamb. The second decanate has a sub-rulership of Leo, the Lion. On March 21st the sun thus enters the decanate of the Lamb, and on the last day of March enters the decanate of the Lion.

About this time of year there is considerable unsettled weather, which has led to the observation that if stormy weather comes early the fine weather will come later, and if the fine weather comes early in March we may look for storms near its end. But there is a more spiritual significance also; for this teaches that those dominated by reason alone—by the head of Aries—should cultivate sympathy, while those guided exclusively by the heart—Leo—need to cultivate the use of the intellect.

The first sign of the zodiac, the Ram, is the exaltation, or finest influence, of the sun; and the second sign, the Bull, is the exaltation of the moon. The sun has ever been symbolized by, and rules over, gold. The fabled Ram of the Golden Fleece, therefore, really signifies the influence represented by the sun in the sign of the Ram. And the Golden Calf—for it could not have been more than a calf when the sun was first born into the sign—signifies the influence of the sun just entering the sign of possessions.

Astronomically the new year is born when the sun crosses the equator to the north and the days become longer than the nights. But the ancients considered, quite logically, that the newborn earth must have a mother (the moon) as well as a father (the sun). Anciently the sun was called Baal or Bel. Both sun and moon were held sacred in different parts of Ireland. In fact, Belfast is supposed to have been named after the old Irish sun-god, Bel.

As all astrologers recognize, the color orange is ruled by the sun; and while the Duke of Orange played his part, nevertheless the law of correspondences plays also a part, so that the Orangemen of Ireland represent in a modern way the ancient faction which discarded the rulership of the moon and paid homage to the sun. Ireland in greater part, however, is ruled by the sign of the Bull, in which the moon exerts its finest power. And the Druids of ancient Ireland commonly are pictured holding the crescent moon in their hands. So also, as all astrologers recognize, green is the color ruled by the moon. Consequently, the Irish who wear the green represent, in the modern way, those who before the advent of Christianity disregarded the rulership of the sun and paid homage to the moon.

The Shamrock

The shamrock is not sacred because, as reputed, St. Patrick picked one to illustrate some theological point but because it represents three trines united at a single point: union of body, soul and spirit on all three planes of existence: physical, astral and spiritual.

The serpent is, and ever has been, the symbol of generation and of wisdom. It tempted Adam and Eve to partake of the Tree of the Knowledge of Good and Evil. And before the advent of Christianity the inhabitants of Ireland understood astrology, and commonly conversed with those on the inner planes of life, as is recorded by their Roman conquerors. Also we have records showing that their Druid priests were well conversant with the laws of generation, by which happiness could be elaborated and finer children be brought into the world. But St. Patrick, followed today by others equally fanatic in the narrowness of their orthodoxy, drove serpents—or true knowledge of Nature's laws—from Ireland, although he was never able to eradicate its symbolism, which was preserved in Ancient Masonry.

St. Patrick's Day

On the 17th of March the sun is in the last decanate of the dark, watery sign Pisces, the natural sign of imprisonment, of inversive forces, and of orthodoxy. This decanate is pictured among the constellations by Cassiopeia, whose arrogant pride, according to Greek mythology, was the cause of beautiful Andromeda (the human soul) being chained to the rock (material interests) for the sensual monster Cetus to devour. In the Bible version, she is represented by Potiphar's wife, who had Joseph placed in jail because he resisted her advances.

The Irish, in celebrating St. Patrick's Day, have chosen that day of the year which anciently was observed as indicating the darkness which precedes the dawn, the pangs of labor preceding the birth of the world on March 21. Thus they unwittingly celebrate their undoing and imprisonment. But the green does hold the hope of release later through the moon's rejuvenating power in the sign of the Bull.

Shrove Tuesday

This festival precedes Easter and occurs just before Lent, while the sun is still in the zodiacal sign of the Man. It is a carnival (and carnival means, "Flesh, fare thee well") in which pancakes play an important part. These pancakes represent the form of the disc of the sun, and in pre-Christian times the Saxons offered the pancakes to the sun as a sacrifice, signifying in this manner the desire to be forgiven their trespasses and to start a period of purification preparatory to a new life at the commencement of the vernal year.

Ash Wednesday

Immediately following Shrove Tuesday, this is the day on which the Saxons threw ashes on all they met, and placed ashes on their foreheads as the symbol of their repentance for sin.

Aquarius, the sign of the Man, in which the sun sojourns at this time, is represented by the key phrase, I Know; and it is only when man attains knowledge of good and evil that he can repent. The baptismal urn figures in this constellation as the cleansing influence prior to a new birth. Wednesday is a Mercury day; Mercury rules intelligence and is exalted in Aquarius. Thus is it shown that moral obligations are accepted. And as referring to their fulfillment, it is the custom in many regions to take the effigy of a man, called "Jack O' Lent," and shoot it full of holes, burn it, or throw it down a chimney. Thus is symbolically indicated the fate awaiting those who, knowing right, follow the inversive path.

Lent

This commences Lent, a period of expiation and penance during the time the sun passes through Pisces, the sign of sorrow and imprisonment, until it is reborn in the sign of the Lamb on Easter.

The sign is pictured by two fishes, and at the time of year when the food store is lowest, having been consumed during the winter and no new crops as yet having had time to grow. Therefore, it is often a time of dearth and famine for agricultural peoples. The herds are famished and too poor for food, and fish is the only available substitute. Lent also symbolizes the psychic purification and material privations that frequently must be undergone to attain spiritual illumination.

Palm Sunday
This is usually the Sunday before Easter, and is said to commemorate the reception of Christ into Jerusalem preceding his death. The sun has triumphantly conquered the Vernal Cross, or is just about to do so, by passing into the sign of the Ram. Virgo, the analytical and scientific sign opposite Pisces, is pictured as holding a palm frond in her uplifted hand as a symbol of information harvested. When Pisces sets, or dies, this symbol rises in the east triumphant. It is, therefore, a day symbolizing not merely the triumph of the sun over the winter—and the human soul over the restrictions of matter—but also of the harvest of intelligence over the darkness of superstition.

Maunday Thursday
On this Thursday, which is the day before Good Friday, it is the custom of those high in office to wash the feet of the poor, a practice similar to the observances of certain sects of the present day at their Love Feasts. Pisces relates to love in that Venus, the planet of love, has its exaltation, or highest influence, there. And this sign Pisces, from which the sun emerges at the commencement of the astronomical year, not only is a watery sign, but rules the feet. It is governed by Neptune, with Jupiter, the planet of Thursday, its co-ruler. The feet symbolize the understanding; and the ceremony thus signifies the understanding of the law of the sacrifice of personal pride for universal good. Pisces is the sign of expiation, as more fully revealed in connection with its tarot card, Major Arcanum XII.

Good Friday
This is a corruption of Gottes Freytag, or God's Friday. It is dedicated to the suffering and burial of the sun god. Friday is the day of Venus. Venus not only is exalted in Pisces, but rules the

marriage sign, Libra. As Good Friday immediately precedes Easter, when the sun is in Aries and the moon past the opposition, the moon has passed over the cross of Libra, on which the sun was crucified the preceding fall, and is in opposition to the sun from the marriage sign. A cross is a marriage of two lines; and in the zodiac the solstitial colure crosses the line where summer and winter are married in the form of a perfect cross. A marriage of sun and moon just preceding Easter is clearly present on Good Friday; Friday, ruled by Venus, being dedicated to affectional affairs.

As indicating the relation of the cross to marriage, all over England Good Friday is ushered in by the cry of "Hot Cross Buns." These are to be found in America also, being biscuits upon the tops of which is traced a cross. Such are called "Bull Cakes" in many countries. Anciently they were offered in Egypt, bous (buns) being the sacred ox, Taurus. In Chaldea they were offered to Astarte, they were offered to Ma by the ancient Mayas of America, were used as Passover cakes by the Jews, and have been found in the ruins of Herculaneum. The circle with the cross in it is even now used by astronomers as the symbol of the earth; and the Bull, exaltation of the moon, is the first earth sign of the zodiac.

Lady's Day

Falling on March 25, this is the day when Gabriel is said to have announced the Immaculate Conception of the Virgin. It was an Egyptian day of festival, however, long before Christian times, and was mentioned by Athanasius before the birth of Christ was fixed by the church to have taken place on December 25. Being the fourth day after the vernal equinox, this date really symbolizes that the sun's forces have become fully polarized to the new cycle; the earth has Realized—the significance of 4—the immaculate rays of the sun from the summer zodiacal signs.

Easter

Easter is a modern adaptation of the old name of the moon, which the Chaldeans called Ishtar, became Astarte to the classical nations, Eoster to the Saxons, and was finally designated by the term now used for her chief annual festival. In this festival her greatest power, as signified by her special exaltation in the beginning of Taurus, is celebrated as chief aid to the function of the sun.

Easter is the first Sunday after the full moon that falls on or next after the 21st of March; if the full moon happens on Sunday, Easter is celebrated one week later. At this full moon, because the sun is in Aries, where its creative energies are strongest, the moon must be in Libra, the sign ruling both marriage and eggs. Eggs, consequently, form a persistent factor in that spring festival dedicated to the redemption of the world by united man and woman, even as it is deemed to be rescued from winter through the offices of the united sun and moon. These eggs commonly are colored in various hues to signify diversity in the expected harvest. They are hidden about and must be hunted for, even as other seeds are placed in the sun-warmed dark ground at the beginning of Taurus, where they germinate, only later to thrust green shoots through the surface into the kindly light of day.

Bunnies also are a part of the ceremony; for although they do not lay eggs, as at Easter children sometimes are led to believe, they are unusually prolific, and symbolize of the power of the earth to bring forth. The Taurus decanate of Taurus, where the moon has her finest power, is pictured in the sky by Lepus, a rabbit, whose outstanding characteristics, in addition to rapidity of reproduction, are fleetness and timidity. The decanate thus pictured is associated with the greatest tragedy mankind has ever known. Hallowe'en, more about which will be found under that heading, commemorates the destruction of the world, the fire, the flood, and the sinking of Atlantis.

The sun at Hallowe'en is in the death decanate of the death sign, Scorpio, directly across the zodiac from this rabbit decanate of Taurus. Thus when Ophiuchus—the man in death-struggle with a serpent who pictures the first decanate of Scorpio—sets in the west, vanquished by the great destruction, Lepus the hare rises in the east, and is shown fleeing, like those who were saved from destruction in Atlantis, as fast as fleet legs will carry him.

The moon, which is so finely situated in this rabbit decanate of Taurus, rules the mentality of man. And it was through a proper application of their minds that those who escaped the world catastrophe were able to avoid the fate of their wicked compatriots. Thus is the rabbit at Easter-time associated with the power of the mind and the power of woman to cooperate in the rescue of the soul from destructive forces, and in its rejuvenation in a more spiritual life.

Easter Monday

The next day after Easter is Easter Monday. It is then the custom in some countries for the leaders of neighboring villages to choose sides and shoot for a calf's head breakfast. The last decanate of the sign of the Ram is the Sagittarius, or Archer, decanate. Sagittarius is pictured in the sky as a huntsman. From the Sagittarius decanate the sun passes into the beginning of the sign of the Bull; hence, the shooting for a breakfast of calf's head. In some other regions the day is celebrated by a hunt.

All Fool's Day

On April 1 the sun has just entered the Lion decanate of the sign of the Ram. The sign pictured by the Lion rules the heart, and that pictured by the Ram rules the head. People who are governed by their hearts alone, with no aid from their heads, commit foolish blunders, just as Phaethon did when he undertook to drive the chariot of the sun through the heavens, and let the prancing steeds run away. And it had been a sorry day on earth, indeed, had not Jove (Jupiter) glanced that way. The frightened horses went tearing toward the earth, the heat drying up the lakes and scorching the plains. Something had to be done if the world was not to be consumed by flames. Jove hurled a thunderbolt from where he sat high on his Olympian throne, and as a bird falls when shot on the wing so was Phaethon dropped into the adjacent Po, the constellated stream now called Eridanus, which pictures the decanate occupied by the sun on All Fool's Day.

This is the day of Huli in Hindoostan where, as in other countries, people are sent on sleeveless errands to instill into their minds that they should use reason and not be led astray by impulse.

May Day

On the 1st of May the sun reaches the harvest, or Virgo, decanate of the first earth sign of the zodiac pictured by the Bull. The Maypole is a phallic emblem relating to the virility and power of the sun. The May Queen represents the earth in a virgin condition (it is the virgin decanate). Thus does the May Pole dance symbolize the immaculate conception of the earth by the paternal rays of the sun, through which the seeds that have been planted in the dark soil are fructified to bring forth an abundant harvest.

In the region where fabled King Arthur is said to have reigned with the knights of his famed Round Table are still to be found cromlechs—concentric circles of stone erected in prehistoric days to portray the orbits of the planets. Thus also do the Maypole dancers portray movements. In fact, the dance as performed by the Mayas of Yucatan leaves no doubt as to what is meant in every particular. The weaving in and out of the dancers as they hold ribbon strands reaching to the central post causes these to form, one with another, sextiles and trines, squares and oppositions, and other aspects by which astrologers ancient and modern plot the harmony or discord reaching the earth from various parts of the heavens.

In Ireland the dancers wear white shirts, and in the Yucatan they clothe themselves entirely in white, to symbolize the purity of conception. And to indicate the result expected, when gestation has been completed and the harvest Virgin has had time to bring forth from the dark soil of earth, it has been the custom during the night to place baskets containing fruit and flowers upon the doorsteps of neighbors.

Ascension Day

This is forty days after Easter; for the sun passes into the Virgo decanate of Taurus before ascending to its heavenly home, even as the soul on earth must garner a mental harvest before it is prepared to function in higher realms. The Bull pictures the sign of fecundity, and the Virgo decanate relates to mental fecundity; for Virgo is a mental sign.

Mother's Day

This is celebrated the second Sunday in May, when commonly the Sun is in the third decanate of the sign of the moon's exaltation, Taurus. The moon, of course, rules the mother principle; but the protective quality of the mother is represented by the constellation Auriga, which pictures this decanate. It shows a charioteer, master of the solar (Sunday) forces, into whose arms has jumped a mother goat, that her two kids, which are with her, may find protection.

Mother's Day thus is not held in honor merely of giving birth but, even as the key word of the last decanate of Taurus is Mastership, to indicate that the function of a true master is to control the forces of Nature and use them for the benefit of those in distress. So the mother, to the extent of her ability, has exercised a similar function in providing for the safety and welfare of her young.

Whit Sunday

This day is said to be observed in commemoration of the descent of the Holy Ghost. Air well symbolizes the Holy Ghost, even as earth symbolizes the physical world. At this time the sun passes from the most fixed of all the earth signs, and the most fertile, pictured by the Bull, into the most volatile of the mental signs, the airy sign Gemini. The descent thus observed symbolizes the application of intelligence to deriving spiritual values from the various experiences which the individual has while on earth.

Father's Day

This day is observed the third Sunday in June when the sun closely approaches the summer solstice. The sun (Sunday) rules the father, and symbolically the power of the father increases until the summer solstice; for the amount of light received by the northern hemisphere is then greatest, at which time the noon position is highest in the heavens, and the father (Sun) is adjacent to the home sign, Cancer.

The Mound Builders of the Mississippi Valley and the Aztecs and Mayas further south built fires on top of their mounds or pyramids at the summer solstice in honor of the virile fatherly power. And the Great Pyramid of Cheops, for the same purpose, was so constructed that on the day of the summer solstice, to anyone looking up the northern side the sun appears as if burning on its top.

Fourth Of July

The sign of the zodiac ruling the home is Cancer. Our Fourth of July is observed to commemorate the establishment of a homeland. On that date the sun, appropriately enough, is in this Cancer sign. We do not celebrate the Fourth with prayer and thanksgiving, but by firing cannon, exploding firecrackers, and other pyrotechnics, both physical and vocal, calling forth expostulations from the press to try to make it more safe and sane. These are all Mars expressions, and on this day the sun has passed into the Mars decanate of Cancer.

Labor Day

One of the common tenets of astrology, ancient and modern, is that the influence of Saturn tends to attract work and heavy responsibilities. When, therefore, those of the olden time wished to comment in terms of universal symbolism upon the importance of labor it is quite consistent that they selected the Saturn decanate of Virgo, the sign of labor. Following the method of universal symbolism still further, which demands that the big influences of life shall be portrayed by equally large pictures, they traced, to represent that labor is essential to all worth while accomplishment, a man of heroic proportions in the sky. Hercules, mightiest of all the laboring men, has a constellation of vast extent.

Our Labor Day has not the same purpose, nor is it celebrated the same, as Labor Day in Europe. Instead, it is a day commemorating the efforts of the common people. The common people are ruled by the moon. Monday is the day of the moon. Consequently, Labor Day is observed on Monday, on the first Monday in September, when the sun has entered the Saturn decanate of the labor sign, pictured in the sky by Hercules. Hercules is not renowned for reciting verses or attending Sunday school; he is famed chiefly for his twelve great labors.

The best quality and the worst quality of any sign express the same general type of energy, but express it through different avenues. It is almost, or quite impossible, to convert the type of energy or the character qualifications denoted by one sign into those denoted by another sign. But it is not a difficult matter to divert the undesirable expression of the energy or character qualifications of any sign into the more desirable expression of the energy or character qualifications of the same sign. This is the work every person should attempt to do, and it is the work which Hercules accomplished.

As there are twelve different signs, representing the deep-seated characteristics of the twelve different types of people, and as Hercules undertook to demonstrate how the worst quality could be diverted into the best quality for each of these types, he had twelve different labors to perform before he had finished. Thus does the observance of a day when the sun is in the section of the zodiac pictured by this great hero offer sage advice to every person as to the most important labor he can accomplish, in addition to paying a high tribute to the tremendous importance of the work of the common people in the world's affairs.

Hallowe'en

On a particular night each year jack-o'-lanterns, white-sheeted figures, black cats, witches on broomsticks, bats, the moon and stars take their place as an accepted part of ceremonies, the most annoying feature of which is the wholesale destruction of property. If such an unusual rite were performed by a single obscure group of people it would seem strange enough, but when we find that the natives of almost every land are doing similar things at the same time it calls for more than a superficial explanation. The moon and stars, which are a part of Hallowe'en decorations, so obviously point to astrology and the prediction of events that no argument need be advanced that this tradition, handed down through the avenue of a worldwide popular custom, is in some manner significant of the position of the heavenly bodies on the night of October 31.

The sun each year on this date is in the death decanate of the death sign of the zodiac, Scorpio. This decanate, or ten-degree section of the zodiac, is pictured in the sky by the constellation Ophiuchus, a man in a life-and-death struggle with a huge serpent. It would seem logical to conclude, therefore, that in some manner men upon earth came to grips with a mighty force, symbolically represented by this starry serpent; that the astrologers had warned them in advance; and that death was intimately associated with the event predicted when it transpired. The greatest number of deaths ever recorded to have taken place at one time is mentioned in an ancient Mayan book written in the Yucatan long after the event.

When the Spanish reached America their priests attempted to destroy every remnant of the writings of the Mayas and the Aztecs. Their histories, astrological treatise, mathematical tables and records were collected and demolished or burned. Only three Mayan books escaped the vigilant eye of Bishop Landa and persist to this day: the Persianus Codex now at the Biblioteque National, Paris; the Dresden Codex, now at the Royal Library at Dresden; and the Tro-Cortesianus Codex, now at the Royal Academy of History, Madrid. These books gave an account, among other things, of the destruction of a continent which had been the homeland from which various centers of civilization throughout the world had been colonized. Into those colonies some of the more enlightened had carried their knowledge of the stellar religion, having been apprised by astrologers that such a catastrophe would occur when the sun, moon and stars would occupy definite relations to one another. That date, so far as the time of year is concerned, is now called October 31.

Here is a quotation from the Tro-Cortesianus:

> In the year 6 Kan, on the 11 Muluc, in the month of Zac, there occurred terrific earthquakes which continued until the 13 Chuen without interruption. The country of the hills of earth—the land of Mu (some translate this Atlantis)—was sacrificed. Twice up-heaved, it disappeared during the night, having been constantly shaken by fires of the underneath. Being confined, these caused the land to rise and sink several times in various places. At last the surface gave way and the ten countries were torn asunder and scattered. They sank with their 64,000,000 inhabitants 8,060 years before the writing of this book.

Tradition holds that this ancient land sank because those who had gained the power to use occult forces no longer devoted them to the welfare of the people, but chiefly to gain selfish advantage. The country had become infested with witches and black magicians, a condition still commemorated by the pictures of witches on broomsticks on Hallowe'en.

A continent sank some 11,000 years ago, and magicians were held responsible for the tragedy, as signified by witches riding high on broom handles. But what about the black cats, always an omen of ill luck? The sign of the zodiac in which the sun has its home is Leo, pictured by a lion. A cat also belongs to the same family of animals and signifies the same zodiacal sign, and was used to indicate the light from the sun. That is, a cat, with its ability to see in the dark, represents knowledge and wise use of the solar creative forces. It was thus the emblem of white magic. But when the cat was black it signified that knowledge and the power of the creative energies were no longer devoted to unselfish ends, but were under the dominion of the power of darkness. A black cat thus became a symbol of black magic, in particular the symbol of the curses dispensed by witches and of the ill luck they were supposed to bring.

Furthermore, at the time of the sinking of the continent, the vernal equinox pointer of the Precessional Cycle had just backed from the sign of the cat, Leo, into the sign of water, Cancer. In fact, this last decanate of Cancer is pictured among the constellations by Argo, the ship in which the wiser ones made their escape from the ill-fated land.

To ward off the ill luck which a black cat signifies, some believe in the potency of a rabbit's foot. Exactly across the zodiac from Ophiuchus, the man wrestling with the curse placed upon him by wicked magicians as indicated by the death-struggle with a serpent, is the constellation Lepus, picturing the rabbit in full flight. It belongs to the first decanate of the sign Taurus. This rabbit in the skies is running away from the place where the struggle is taking place, in fact, he is just as far from it as he can get, as were those wise ones who, warned by their understanding of astrology, left the ancient land before the cataclysm occurred. The foot is a symbol of understanding, and as symbolic of the power of understanding to save its possessor from a "jinx," the rabbit's foot still is in high favor.

The bats on our Hallowe'en decorations, because such creatures dislike to face the light, hiding away in dark caves during the day and hunting their prey only at night, are symbols of the iniquitous forces of darkness, the elemental messengers which are sent forth by witches and magicians to carry out their nefarious work. All this is very gruesome; but it relates to the most terrible disaster that has been experienced by mankind, although other cataclysms are to be expected each precessional cycle when the vernal equinox backs from Leo into Cancer, and from Aquarius into Capricorn.

The Aztecs, apparently having lost the knowledge of this large cycle, but retaining the knowledge that the year within the larger cycle could be determined from their 52-year period, observed the night of the closing of this period with abject terror. This 52-year period was called Xihuitmolpia, and they held, from sound astrological considerations, that the destruction of a portion of the world would occur on the closing night of one of these 52-year periods. On the last night of the period, therefore, all fires were extinguished and the inhabitants moved out of the city to the tops of the surrounding hills to await anxiously either for destruction or the coming of dawn. If the sun rose in the morning it signified there would be no cataclysm for another 52 years at least, and all went back to their homes rejoicing.

The tradition is that many persons were taken out of their bodies in a single night at the time the old continent was destroyed, and that some of these, especially those wicked and devoted to the black arts, were unable to make quick and proper adjustment to the next life plane and, being earth-bound, remained adjacent to the earth. These shades that still walked the earth after the cataclysm of October 31 are represented by the jack-o'-lanterns and white sheeted figures of our day. With the same significance the Australian Bushmen paint white stripes over their ribs and limbs to represent skeletons, and spend the night dancing in the firelight.

Among the people of many countries, such as the French of Paris, it is still the custom at this time to place food on the graves of the dead. Those taken violently from the body, especially those of coarse appetites, do not change their desires immediately. They yet crave the foods to which they have become accustomed. And tradition holds that when the continent sank the survivors placed food before the dead that they might draw from its aromas sufficient electromagnetic energy to assuage their craving.

The following two days were largely devoted by those yet on the physical plane who possessed the proper knowledge of spiritual laws in assisting those who had died to become reconciled and readjusted to the new life where they now found themselves. Thus do we have, following Hallowe'en, All Saint's Day and All Soul's Day, given to observances commemorating the passage to the next life, and to prayers for the dead.

The most outstanding feature of the Hallowe'en ceremony is, of course, the making of a terrific noise and the destruction of as much property as can be done without reprisal from the authorities. This racket is the expression of man's racial memory of the noise which accompanied the great catastrophe; and the destruction of things and the mischief wrought are pantomime representations of the destruction of a continent of old.

The Mayas and other peoples had more definite knowledge than the later Aztecs of the astronomical factors which coincide with such vast upheavals as Hallowe'en celebrates. These astronomical factors are set forth, with reference to the destruction of Sodom and Gomorrah and other allied things, in Brotherhood of Light Course VII, *Spiritual Astrology*, lessons Nos. 76 and 82.

Thanksgiving Day

This day is established each year by presidential proclamation. To be normal it must take place during the time the sun is in the Sagittarius decanate of Sagittarius, a sign denoting religion, and the decanate whose key word is Devotion. Prayer is an essential part of the Thanksgiving ceremony.

Rightfully observed, it falls about four weeks before Christmas. Holidays are periods when people take short vacations from work and spend more than the usual amount of money. Falling so near Christmas, people have hardly recovered from spending Thanksgiving money before the Yuletide holidays are upon them. Therefore, merchants in the U.S. during the third term of office of Franklin Delano Roosevelt brought pressure to bear upon him to change Thanksgiving so from that time on it would fall several weeks earlier. They held, and widely proclaimed, that this would be good for business. But even though for a year or two the President did thus proclaim Thanksgiving to be several weeks earlier, the attempt to hold the festival on an inappropriate astrological day—for the sun was then in Scorpio, which is hardly a thanksgiving sign—was a failure. In some states two Thanksgivings were held, one on the day proclaimed by the President, and one on the accustomed day which was thus designated by the Governor of the state. In other states people were indifferent to a Thanksgiving Day which they felt somehow was not right. And thus in spite of the efforts of the merchants, supported by the efforts of the President, there was a drifting back to the proper astrological day.

The first decanate of the sign Sagittarius is pictured in the sky by the constellation Lyra, the harp. Such a harp it was the ancient custom to play when singing songs of praise and thanksgiving to the Creator. Sagittarius is pictured among the constellations as the Huntsman; and the Turkey, which is so notable a part of the Thanksgiving ritual, is native to America and was obtained by hunting. Thanksgiving hunts still are popular.

A good word for the influence of Jupiter, the planet ruling Sagittarius, is abundance; and thus the festive board on this day, more than any other, is made to groan with the richness and variety of the viands. Second in importance only to the largest of American game birds, the turkey, the rotund beaming face of the pumpkin pie looks up from its place as the countenance of Jove himself. In astrological lore it is commonly acknowledged that Jupiter people like good things to eat and an abundance of them. And thus the table on this day is explained. But what significance has the public prayer?

Jupiter, ruler of the sign where the sun is found on this day, is called the Greater Benefic, the planet whose influence brings the best in fortune. He also is the planet ruling that group of desires, called the Religious Urges, which encourage prayer. Because deliverance from poverty and privation is so frequently associated with the things he rules astrologically, it is the more fitting that his day, Thursday, and his sign, Sagittarius, should be chosen for offering thanks.

Not only does the day persist, due to the astral pressure which makes such expression most easy on this day of the year, when special prayers of thanksgiving are offered, but this same vibratory relation occasioned by the position of the sun along its zodiacal path gives carrying power to such thoughts that makes them more than ordinarily effective. It is the special time of year in which our minds most readily tune in, through feelings of devotion and gratitude, on benevolent intelligences of the inner plane. Currents of astral force of astral origin set in the direction most favorable to carry human prayers for security and welfare to those on the inner plane who best are fitted to give such aid.

The answer to prayer of necessity requires an agent. Material food, for instance, is not created out of nothing and deposited in our larder by the Divine Mind. If it reaches our table, some human agency has played a part. And to an extent not commonly recognized, those who have passed from physical life, yet who are tuned in on through kindred interests, through aspiration, or through the avenue of prayer to the Most High, are able to assist those yet on earth to solve their problems; and through still other agencies to gain for them the comforts for which praise is offered on Thanksgiving Day.

Christmas

The very first glance at a chart picturing all 48 of the ancient constellations brings to the attention that two of the constellations, quite far apart in the sky, portray the same mythological creatures. Part horse and part man, the only difference between Centaurus, which pictures the Sagittarius decanate of Leo, where the sun may be found from August 3 to August 13, and Sagittarius, which pictures the sign where the sun may be found from November 22 to December 22, is that Centaurus is armed with a shield and spear, while Sagittarius has a cloak and uses bow and arrow.

This identity of the pictured forms at once suggests that the ancients who placed these pictures in the sky to convey information in terms of universal symbolism, desired that these two sections of the heavens be closely linked in the teaching they wished to give. It certainly is not coincidence that one larger and one smaller section of the zodiac should be represented by similar creatures; or that those chosen should indicate the human qualities carried by a horse. Rather, especially as the huntsman and the spearman face as if each were traveling toward the place of the other, it signifies that there is a movement of the same type of influence from one station in the zodiac to the other.

We are bound to infer, therefore, that the teaching signified, and the traditional story left to give more detail include, a movement, and carrying from one place to another—else why the horses' legs?—and that its comprehension requires several stations in the zodiac, the two most important being those pictured by the roving horsemen.

If we follow the simplest and most obvious method, which is always that employed by those who traced these doctrines in the sky, it will lead us to commence with Sagittarius because it pictures 30 degrees, and is therefore more important than Centaurus which pictures only 10 degrees of space. We may be sure, however, that a child or children will play a part in the story, because the smaller influence relates to the middle decanate of Leo, which has natural rule of children.

Sagittarius, ruled by Jupiter, and the Sagittarius decanate of Leo, also having Jupiterian rule, are known to relate to gifts. Astrologers say that what Jupiter brings comes freely as the result of goodwill rather than through work as is the case with Saturn. Hence it is that immediately after the sun leaves the Sagittarius sign in winter is the time when gifts are given. Christmas is not on the day when the sun reaches its farthest declination south, which is the day when it crosses from the manger of the horse to the manger of the goat, because for three days it remains at this lowest, most southern point before starting to bring back new life and light into the world.

Giving it three days' grace after December 22 ensures that on Christmas Day the sun will be moving northward in declination, and that the days will have started to get longer. They will thus continue to lengthen until June 22, when the sun reaches the topmost point of the home sign, Cancer. The topmost part of a home commonly is the chimney. Therefore the sun, in coming to the home from the place where Jupiter brings his gifts, on the line dividing Sagittarius and Capricorn in winter, must touch it first at the highest spot, the chimney. And to reach it, of course, he comes through the air.

In vain you will search the Bible for any mention of Christmas tree or Santa Claus. Yet that they are linked traditionally with the Centaur picturing the middle decanate of the section of the heavens relating to children seems certain. For on that day when they are prominent, it is said a child was born—born in a stable underground as the sun yet represents. It has reached its lowest point when between the horse and goat, from which time it starts to gain new strength.

Santa Claus, like the horsemen in the sky, one of which relates to the time of winter's cold and the other to the heat of summer, portrays two seasons of the year. His garb is chiefly red; for as representing the constellated Centaur is he not next the fiery furnace, Crater, where the heat glows fiercest? Yet also, to denote the snow of winter, the trimming of the garb is spotless white. The gifts he brings at Christmastime are tokens of still greater gifts to come. They are the promise that abundance will follow after the time of winter dearth, when the heat from the sun will have had time to ripen crops again. Still ahead, even though the days have started in their lengthening, is a period of privation and cold. Stored supplies may become exhausted, giving rise to dark despair; yet even at the entrance of this period does he give promise of better days to come.

In his jovial manner and rotund figure he expresses the Jupiterian quality of Sagittarius, from which the sun has just moved at Christmas. This is a sign of religion. And even as Santa Claus brings promise of material gifts, so religion brings an equal cheer and promise of spiritual blessings after the hard dark days of earth are done. Yes, the days are darkest about Christmastime. They are like those other days when hope so fades that nothing seems worth while. Therefore is it fitting that there should be joyous news of a happy future life.

Santa, however, not merely represents Jupiter's winter sign, but also a decanate of Leo, sign ruled by the sun. And anyone who has viewed the radiant rising sun on a cold and frosty morning will remember the resemblance to Santa's red circle of a face. Yet the youngsters of the land, whose special joy he is, would not recognize the rotund fellow if divested of his whiskers. They are an essential part of his makeup because at Christmas time the sun has just moved into Capricorn, and chin whiskers are the special adornment of a goat.

Horses customarily draw sleighs. Therefore, Sagittarius and Centaurus well could qualify; but as still more significant of the cold bleak winter days, reindeer are now used to take their place. They are more accustomed to ice and snow. Before this sleigh—which coming from Sagittarius, the Jupiterian sign of abundance, is filled with good things to overflowing—can get to the fireplace, Crater, it must land on top of the house at Cancer. And thus really does the sun. For after touching the highest point it reaches, which is where it enters the home sign Cancer, it immediately starts descending, as if going down the chimney, until it passes into the decanate pictured by Crater. It does not tarry in this fireplace, or hottest decanate of the zodiac, however, but at once moves into the decanate pictured by Centaurus, the other horseman of the sky.

The feet, it is true, are ruled by Pisces. But ask any small boy or girl—such as is ruled by the Leo section of the sky—if it is enough to hang up the mere feet of stockings on Christmas evening. If I remember rightly, there is usually a hunt for stockings that are long and ample, such as come well up on the thighs. And it is the legs thus covered by the longer hosiery that Sagittarius rules, and of which its decanate in Leo also must partake.

The horseman of Leo is not the gift, but the one who brings it; for it is the sun at this time of year that ripens the grain in the field and the fruit on the trees. The gifts which the traveler from the north thus brings, while related to the children of Leo, are pictured in the next sign to it, in the harvest sign, Virgo. It is really the Virgin Mother, not Santa Claus, from whom the gifts more directly come. The lady of the sky holds a palm frond in one hand and heads of wheat in the other; while Hercules, who pictures the middle decanate of the Virgo sign, holds in his hand the branch of a tree adorned with fruit. The fruit thus shown is the fulfillment of the promise made at the time when the nights were longest, just as the sun turns back from its farthest distance away. This promise was not made by using a tree when it was filled with fruit; because such are hard to find at Christmastime. It was made by using a tree symbolic of perpetual life, by using an evergreen tree. The fruit to come, when ripened through the heat of the sun in Leo, was represented by presents on that tree. And it was spangled with stars and bedecked with lights as a token that the sun, thus moving through the firmament, was on the way to dissipate the winter's darkness.

At this yuletide time of year, still further to connect the passing of the sun from Sagittarius to the Centaurus decanate of Leo, the sign of love affairs and pleasure, it is the custom to hang mistletoe with the privilege of kissing whomsoever passes under it. The mistletoe, like the Christmas tree, is of evergreen foliage, and thus symbolically promises everlasting life. But because it grows above the earth, apparently too pure and holy to touch the physical soil, it came to have a special spiritual significance. Its berry fruit, formed without polluting contact with the loam of earth, came to be looked upon as derived from an immaculate conception.

Kissing under the mistletoe, even in times not remote, was a solemn and binding ceremony. It was the token of a chaste affection and the promise of marriage. More than that, it was the promise that out of the love then expressed should develop a new and more spiritual type of life. Such a life of spiritual endeavor, as Santa Claus and Centaurus clearly teach, is dependent upon what is done for others. It is the effort to give, rather than the effort to take, which promises a spiritual harvest. After all, in the realms of the future, after we shall have passed from this mundane sphere, the physical objects men set their hearts upon will have less value than the tinsel and gilded baubles with which they decorate the Christmas tree.

The Saturnalia

In olden times many of the eastern nations had a year of 360 days, one day for each degree of the zodiac. They were aware, however, that there were 365 days in the year, and to account for this they sliced five days just before January 1 from their year, and completely ignored it for business purposes. Because at that time the sun had entered Capricorn, the home of Satan (Saturn), these days were devoted to the Saturnalia, which was really a festival to the devil. At that time, in some countries, licentiousness and debauchery ran riot; as is well attested in the history of Rome.

The day of Satan, also—that is, Saturday—because of the reputation of its ruler, was mostly considered a day of ill omen. Julius

Caesar in B.C. 46 reformed this more ancient calendar, and Pope Gregory XIII made further improvement in A.D. 1582. Yet at present the last days of the year are considered a part of the Yuletide season.

Chapter 8

A Prophecy for the Aquarian Age

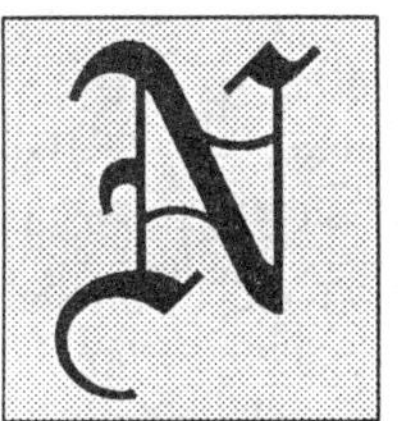o one will be so bold as to deny that the seasons are caused by the apparent movement of the sun through the 12 signs of the zodiac. No one will dispute the statement that we habitually expect certain conditions when the sun is in some signs of the zodiac that we do not have when it is in others. We do not expect, for instance, to harvest wheat each month of the year, nor do we plant the same crops during all months. And, as all must know, the months are merely the effect of the sun as it apparently passes through the zodiacal signs.

When each spring the sun apparently crosses the celestial equator, the days become longer than the nights. This is both the beginning of the astronomical year and the commencement of the zodiac; and it is called the Vernal Equinox. From this point, wherever it may be among the stars, the sun starts its annual pilgrimage. Each 30 degrees covered from this point marks one zodiacal sign, and 360 degrees of apparent travel bring it back at the end of the year to the vernal equinox again.

Cause of the Precessional Cycle

But due to the fact that the earth is flattened at the poles, giving it a bulge at the equator which makes the gravitational pull of the sun and planets on the earth stronger there, and that the inclination of this bulging equator of the earth to the plane of the ecliptic where the gravitational pull is strongest is $23° 26' 50''$, the earth also undergoes a slow gyratory motion. Just as a top which is spinning swiftly (to represent the daily rotation of the earth), if not perpendicular to the surface on which it rests will slowly move its upper part in a small circle, so performs the rotating earth. It may take the top but a single minute to make one complete gyratory circle, but it takes the earth 25,868 years. This gyratory motion of the earth, due to the gravitational pull on its leaning and bulging equator, causes the point where the sun in spring crosses the celestial equator (which is the projection in the sky of the earth's equator) slowly to move backward through the constellated stars.

This backward movement of the vernal equinox, by which the commencement of the astronomical year and the commencement of the zodiacal signs move through the circle of constellated stars in 25,868 years, has nothing whatever to do with the movement of the sun around some center. It relates to a movement of the earth which can be demonstrated in a laboratory by means of a gyroscope, and commonly is called The Precession of the Equinoxes.

As the sun acts as the pointer indicating the influence of each sign of the zodiac on life during the one-twelfth of the year it is in a sign, so the vernal equinox, or place of the sun at the commencement of each year, acts as a pointer indicating the influence of each sign of the zodiac on life during the one-twelfth of the Great Cycle the equinox is in a sign. The precessional cycle is as truly measured by the apparent position of the sun as is the common year; but it is measured from a fixed point among the stars, which the common year is not, and each 30 degrees from the starting point instead of measuring the influence covering a month of time, measures the influence of the zodiacal sign during one-twelfth of the precessional year of 25,868 common years, or 2,156 common years. Each such period of 2,156 common years during which the vernal equinox backs through one successive 30 degrees from the stellar starting point is called an Age.

The Aquarian Age Commenced in 1881

It is disappointing that there is no undisputed record of the date when the first of Aries among the constellations and the first of Aries among the zodiacal signs exactly coincided. We cannot select the western boundary of the constellation Aries for this purpose, for no one at this day knows precisely where that boundary is located among the stars, or even if the picture on maps today is of the same size and outline as it was in olden times. Thus there is no precise astronomical observation by which it can be determined when any of the ages began.

The astronomers say that the vernal equinox right now is still well within the constellation Pisces. And they are quite correct in saying this. But the signs of the zodiac, whether considered from the standpoint of the sun's annual cycle, or from the standpoint of the Great Cycle of the equinox, are not of the same extent as the constellations. We do not limit the sign Cancer to but 15 degrees along the ecliptic, nor do we give to the sign Virgo some 50 degrees along the ecliptic, although the constellations bearing those names have about such extent. Constellations merely picture the influence of the signs, and were not designed either to denote the position nor the extent along the zodiac of the influence they thus explained.

To be consistent with all astrological doctrine, each sign must extend along the path of the sun just 30 degrees. Wherever that point may be among the stars, 30 degrees back from the star which marks the starting point of the Great Cycle is the end of Aquarius; just as 30 degrees back of where the sun crossed into Aries, regardless of stellar positions, this year or any other year, marks the end of the sign Aquarius.

It is possible to cite the 1881 pyramidal inches in the Grand Gallery of the Great Pyramid, that 1881 gives the double 9, or 18, by which the ancients designated the larger cycles, various prophecies, and other indications that the Aquarian Age really commenced in the year 1881.

When in natal astrology, however, we have a birthchart which has not been precisely timed, we resort to comparing the events which have happened in the life with the positions found in the chart, and with the progressed aspects. Therefore, as there is no certain starting point among the stars, or any other astronomical data to ascertain the commencement of the Aquarian Age, it seems better to observe when events which clearly are not of the Pisces type began to be prevalent; for during the preceding 2,156 years the equinox pointer was moving back from the first of constellated Aries through the sign Pisces.

It should not be necessary to point out that the world has now moved from a state in which the emphasis was placed on Belief, which is the key word for Pisces, to one in which it places chief reliance on Knowledge, which is the key word of Aquarius. Aquarius is a scientific sign, and since 1881 science has made greater advances than during the whole 2,156 preceding Piscean years. Uranus, the ruler of Aquarius, governs invention, psychology, electricity and the study of the stars. It has only been since 1881 that the world has adopted electricity as an important source of power, that electric lighting has made night work almost as convenient as day work, that inventions have revolutionized industry, that astronomy has extended its boundaries from our solar system to the measurement of stars and other universes, and that psychology has come to be recognized as a subject that should be taught in our schools.

People born under the sign Aquarius are progressive, humanitarian, keen students of psychology, given to investigating psychical phenomena, and quickly take an interest in astrology. As a similar influence on a world scale should be expected when the equinox is in Aquarius, we may be sure that it was not without significance that the New Thought movement, Christian Science, Mental Science, Theosophy and what-not, had their birth not far from 1881. The first organized effort by scientific men to investigate psychical phenomena, for instance, was commenced with the founding in 1882 of the Society for Psychical Research, an effort which has continued with great success up to the present time. We may be sure also that at no distant date the facts of astrology, the facts of extra sensory perception, the facts of induced emotion and the facts of directed thinking will be taught in the public schools. Labor organizations are ruled by Uranus, which governs the Aquarian sign, and since 1881 these have gained in power, bringing improved living conditions among the poorer classes. Within a century people will look back with horror on the time when any man willing to work was denied a livelihood.

Considering from the evidence, which each day is before all eyes, that we have emerged from the water and now are in the air, through which presently all will travel, and over which, figuratively speaking, we receive daily our radio programs, let us recognize that "I Believe," which was sufficient for the Piscean Era must now gradually give way to the Aquarian thirst for Knowledge. Pisces rules imprisonment, Aquarius governs friendship. Both physical and mental fetters belong to the past, and in the near future not only will man's mind be freed from bondage to sacerdotalism, but he no longer will be imprisoned for crime; he will be scientifically treated for his moral maladies, not punished for them.

Pisces is a watery sign, and during its reign we conquered the ocean and made steam our slave; but not until Aquarius gained the day did we vanquish the air and harness the electrical current. Not only is Aquarius an airy sign, but Uranus, its planet, rules electricity and electromagnetic force. In the very near future the electromagnetic rays of the sun will be utilized as cheap motive power. Aquarius also has special rule over astrology, and soon all men will recognize that the rays from the various planets impinge upon their finer bodies and constantly stimulate them to corresponding actions. Knowing this, it will be but a step to learn how, through induced emotion and directed thinking, and taking advantage of the vibratory radiations from objects, they may utilize, divert into selected channels, and give the desired constructive trend to any given planetary influence. Thus will they come to accept The Religion of the Stars.

The Religion of the Stars not only embraces astrology, extrasensory perception, induced emotion and directed thinking, but includes the use of extra sensory perception to communicate with those who have passed through death to the inner plane. Aquarius is pictured as a man in the sky pouring water down upon the earth, where a fish drinks it joyfully. The water symbolizes the wisdom which flows from the great minds of those who have passed to the spirit plane of life, and which may be utilized to quench the thirst of our souls through conscious mental communion.

To those who wish startling and conclusive evidence of the communion between the discarnate and the incarnate, as observed by trained minds, there are in most public libraries such books as *Dawn of the Awakened Mind,* by Dr. John King, founder and president of the Canadian Society of Psychical Research, and the works of Sir Oliver Lodge, Camille Flammarion, Sir Arthur Conan Doyle, Rev. G. Vale Owen, Hill, Leaf, Watson, Stead and a score of others. Better still, let the investigator develop Intellectual ESP until without negative mediumship or objectional phases of psychism, he can carry on such communication himself. Yet as Uranus governs high frequency radiations and delicate apparatus, the Aquarian Age will not advance far until someone will invent a purely mechanical gadget for such between the planes communication, and it will become as common, and no more mysterious, than is the radio today.

We Are in the Libra Decanate of the Aquarian Age

Each zodiacal sign is divided into three decanates of ten degrees each. And just as the twelve zodiacal constellations each picture the influence and significance of one of the twelve zodiacal signs, so is each decanate of the zodiac pictured in its influence and significance by one of the 36 ultra-zodiacal constellations. Thus is the Libra decanate of Aquarius, into which the equinox backed in 1881, explained in symbolical pictograph by Cetus, the Whale-Monster in the sky.

Libra is the zodiacal sign of marriage, and the Libra decanate of each airy sign carries with it some of this significance. While the equinox was in Pisces, woman was in bondage to marital relations. But no sooner did the equinox move into the Libra decanate of Aquarius than she began to struggle for equal rights with man. Libra, as astrologers well know, rules equality, justice, partnership and marriage. Already under this new influence in world affairs, woman has in many regions gained privileges heretofore granted only to men. And all in due time she will gain equal suffrage and equal economic rights, not merely in a few countries, but throughout the world.

As Libra is the marriage sign, under this decanate influence man has been persuaded to study the laws of sex, all too long neglected. The Whale Monster, which explains the decanate, relates to persecution and repression, and in a wider sense to the destructive power of discord. In Greek mythology, Perseus, symbolizing the enlightened mind of man, slew this symbol of discordant might and rescued fair Andromeda. Already we have the work of Freud and other psychoanalysts, revealing the damage so often done by sex repression and other submerged emotions. Gradually it is being recognized, as taught in Brotherhood of Light courses V, *Esoteric Psychology*, and IX, *Mental Alchemy*, how these and other destructive forces within the unconscious mind can be reconditioned so as to express, no longer discordantly, but through constructive channels, and thus rescue the individual from his previous misfortune-attracting bondage.

Also through better understanding of the law of sex, gradually will be eradicated the greatest evil on the face of the earth today, loveless marriage. And in this understanding, electromagnetic relations and mental trends as mapped by birthchart and progressed planets will play their part, and guide the endeavors which will free many souls from the necessity of functioning through unhealthy bodies. In mythology there is closely associated with Cetus, as the symbol of discord, the old bondage of the Piscean Age. Andromeda, picturing one of the decanates of Pisces, was chained to a rock because of the arrogant pride of her mother, queen of dark Ethiopia. And it was chaotic Neptune, ruler of this sign of imprisonment who, when she was thus chained to the rock of atheistic materialism, sent the largest and most ominous creature of the zodiac, Cetus, to devour her.

Aquarius is a scientific sign, and encourages the invention of mechanical contrivances, some of which tend to prolong life and some of which are tremendously destructive. In our seats of learning many of those who place reliance on the demonstrated knowledge ruled by Aquarius, which has displaced the Piscean reliance on belief, have jumped to the conclusion that the physical is the whole of life, and that the universe possesses no guiding intelligence. These atheistic materialists, who occupy prominent positions in our universities and important sections of the press, are determined to impose their convictions on all the world. Scholastic dictators, in the arrogance and pride of their purely physical accomplishments, take the part of Queen Cassiopeia and bind Andromeda—the collective soul of the human race—to the rock of atheistic materialism. So determined are they that the public shall receive no proof of life after death, of astrology, or of any superphysical power that, like Neptune in the Greek story, that they resort to persecution when they find anyone opposing their chaotic and wholly unwarranted views.

Yet this very atheistic materialism, to bind humanity to which the scholastic dictators spend the best energies of their lives and resort to distortion of the truth and wholesale suppression of facts, is that which attracts to mankind the monster which most threatens humanity's destruction. Where this doctrine gains a foothold—the doctrine that there is no power above the physical, and no life beyond the tomb—we find people easily led by those who, violating every sense of human decency, and quite devoid of reluctance to cause untold suffering, act on the belief that the spoils of the world belong to those who can marshal the greatest force.

In the hands of these materialistic atheists, the science of the Aquarian Age is but a means to acquire new and greater implements of destruction. The rock of materialism, representing the physical world to which scholastic dictators would bind the human race, is washed by the waves of racial prejudice and jealous passions; and it cannot fail repeatedly to plunge the world into increasingly horrible wars. And mankind can be rescued from this annihilating fate only by winged Perseus, the enlightened mind of a humanity which recognizes a higher plane, as did the hero when he came from the air to slay huge Cetus, and which acts as did he, from other than self-interest and material motives.

The Seven Sections of the Aquarian Age

Another division of each precessional sign, not so generally known but well recognized by the ancients, is of a septenary nature. It was stated in veiled form by Abbot Trithemius, was mentioned later by Eliphas Levi, and was made plain by T. H. Burgoyne. By this method each sign is divided into seven equal sections, each section being ruled by one of the seven naked-eye planets in the regular planetary hour order of their succession. That is, the Sun always rules the first section of an Age, then comes the Venus section, the Mercury section, the Moon section, the Saturn section, the Jupiter section, and finally Mars ruling the last section of the Age. As the equinox passes through Aquarius in 2,156 years, it takes 308 years for it to move through one of these septenary divisions.

Now glance at the history of Greece during the Mars section of the Arian Age—that is, from 583 B.C. to 257 B.C. Only one year after the commencement of this section of the Age the Pythian (Mars) games were instituted at Delphi, and during the 308 years that followed there was a constant succession of military achievements, including those of Alexander the Great. It was not until five years before the ending of this era that the first meeting took place between the Greek phalanx and the Roman legion. In the very year, 275 B.C., when the Mars section gave way to the Sun section of the following Piscean Age, Pyrhus was beaten by the Romans under Curius Dentatus at Beneventum; and from this victory dates the supremacy of Rome in Italy, and the commencement of her power, which before the end of this Sun section of the Piscean Age in 33 A.D. was to dominate the then-known world.

The Mars section of the Piscean Age extended from 1573 to 1881. Passing over the wars, we note that this was the period when machinery (ruled by Mars) came into use, and during which iron ships, steam engines, and mechanical contrivances for greater destruction in warfare were invented. In 275 B.C., when the equinox entered the Sun section of the Piscean Age and the section of Mars ended, there was no cessation of war. The Sun recognizes no equal; he must rule supreme. There was, therefore, an incessant struggle for world dominion on the part of Rome.

Starting about 1881 when the Sun section of the Aquarian Age started, we find Germany determined to play the same role in this age that Rome played in the last one. She started teaching her people that it was their destiny to rule the world, and 33 years later, in 1914, she launched World War I in the effort thus to acquire world domination.

The material of this Chapter thus far given was published and copyrighted in Brotherhood of Light publication entitled, *A Prophecy for the Aquarian Age,* before the start of the Pluto Period; and in view of subsequent events we will quote verbatum what was said in the closing paragraphs of that article:

> In that war Germany was defeated, but let us not blind ourselves to the disagreeable fact that over and over again, until world dominion by some single government or by some single type of government is accomplished, other aggressive nations will seek to gain the power which so recently drenched the world with blood. It will be tried in Europe. But the greatest danger lies in the nation which flaunts the rising sun as the emblem on the flag her soldiers so willingly follow to glory and to death. That nation is Japan.
>
> Under this Sun section of the Aquarian Age, representative democracy and totalitarian forms of government cannot persist side by side. Sooner or later, and after great strife, the whole world will adopt, or be forced to accept, a single governmental standard. Aquarius is a democratic sign; but this is an imperialistic section of the Age, and the only hope for the world to escape complete servitude to an Oriental power dominated by Japan is through recognition of the principle of equal opportunities and individual liberties which is characteristic of Aquarius as a whole, and the cooperative upholding of that principle with sufficient force, as did Perseus, to slay, when necessary, Cetus, the greedy and mighty monster of armed aggression.
>
> What that form of government will be which before many years will encompass the whole world depends upon the intelligence, integrity and courage of our representative democracies which, with all their present faults, exemplify the finest quality of

Aquarius. But of this we may be sure, one general form of government alone will encircle and be the dominant political force of the globe.

Now let us proceed to material not published in the original article; for at that time, while it was recognized there must be ten orbs in a chain, and the general attributes of the tenth orb were set forth in spiritual astrology, in mythology and in the tarot, it was not known when the planet would be discovered.

The Pluto Period Arrives

From time to time, and making precise predictions as to world affairs more difficult, there are new and unheralded astronomical phenomena. Hitherto unknown comets flash across the solar system, new stars suddenly blaze into brilliance, and even new planets are discovered. When we go back in history we find that the discovery of a new planet has always, as now, heralded worldwide changes.

Uranus, the planet of invention and independence, was discovered in 1781, and may rightly be said to have ushered in the machine age, and the age of the republics, which now so desperately need defending. The looms of England, under the new impetus, rapidly transformed her from an agricultural into an industrial nation. Engines of all kinds came into use, one invention following another. Eventually electricity, even more closely allied with Uranus, added its power to this age of manufacture.

In 1782 the Peace of Versailles and Paris granted an independent existence to the United States. This set a precedent to be followed by most of the countries of the New World. The representative democratic form of government came to be a dominant factor in all the Western Hemisphere.

Then in 1846 Neptune was discovered, ushering in the age of oil and gas, which prepared the way for our present industrial system and our present means of locomotion. Automobiles can run on steam, although gas has proved better; but flying, ruled by Neptune, has been made possible through the light weight engines developing tremendous power and using gas.

Neptune also brought into the world a new religious conception, that of modern spiritualism. Before the Fox Sisters and their rappings in 1848, similar phenomena were recognized, but were deemed to be witchcraft and the works of the devil. Modern

Spiritualism had its birth on March 31, 1848, at Hydesville, N.Y., and gave to the world scientific proof that the soul survives the dissolution of the body.

In 1848 there were revolutions in France, Germany, Italy and Austria-Hungary. And gold was discovered in California, which opened up an entire new section of the world. This age of oil also ushered in a new method of financing business, the method by which many individuals could pool their resources. Instead of individual enterprises and partnerships with their limited ability to raise capital, corporations, composed of share holders, came to be the dominant factor in the business and industrial world.

And now we come to the planet Pluto, discovered only a few months after the collapse of the stock market in November 1929, and the commencement of the greatest financial depression the world has ever known. As data given in the newspapers often is not precise, and as such data often becomes obscured through the passage of time, this matter was referred to Dr. Robert G. Aitken, Director Emeritus of Lick Observatory, for the sake of correct recording. According to this authority, Pluto was discovered January 21, 1930, on photographic plates, was further checked (period of delivery), and then announced to the general public on March 12, 1930 (date of its birth).

The Pluto Period of the Sun Section of the Libra Decanate of the Aquarian Age already has brought outstanding developments and tremendous changes characteristic of this most newly discovered planet. Pluto rules the inner plane and the inside of things, encourages group activity, has two trends, one constructive and the other destructive, exerts an influence toward splitting groups into opposing factions, and is never milk-and-water but favors drastic action. The Upper-Pluto influence tends toward cooperation and spirituality. The Lower-Pluto influence tends toward racketeering, coercion, dictatorship and the domination of others through fear and force.

Within the United States, racketeering developed during the prohibition era, reaching its peak the very year Pluto was discovered. In 1934 the G-Men, meeting force and organization with still more effective force and cooperation, had the gangsters and kidnapers on the run.

Then came a split in the labor movement, and one of the two factions contended for national power. The C.I.O., by the first of

1937, was employing typical Lower-Pluto methods against employers. The sitdown strike, in which employees took over and refused to leave the property where they worked, reached its peak in January, 1937.

Pluto's Influence on Occult Knowledge

When the Brotherhood of Light lessons were written, a vast amount of observation and experimentation had been done by outstanding scientific men relative to the various types of psychical phenomena. And as much was even then known about electromagnetism, these phenomena could be, and were, correctly explained in the lessons in terms of modern science.

The Society for Psychical Research was founded in 1882, at the commencement of the Aquarian Age, for the express purpose of "making an organized and systematic attempt to investigate the large group of phenomena designated by such terms as mesmeric, psychical, and Spiritualistic." From time to time many of the most outstanding men in the scientific world joined this group and assisted in collecting authentic instances of clairvoyance, prevision, telepathy, psychometry, levitation, etherealization, materialization and other types of psychic phenomena, and in conducting experiments under the most exacting conditions to determine whether these phenomena actually take place. Their published reports confirm that they do take place.

But in spite of the tremendous volume of evidence set forth by these men of high scientific standing, other academic individuals wedded to materialism were able by ridicule and propaganda to cause the public to ignore the proofs of psychic phenomena, and the books containing the proofs, one after another, went out of print. They were never given the wide circulation which the tremendous importance of their subject matter warranted.

Then in 1934, immediately after the publication of the last of the 210 Brotherhood of Light lessons, Duke University published the first statistical (Pluto) work on extra sensory perception. In the six years from 1934 to 1940, Duke University Laboratory reported 999,674 trials, and other university laboratories following similar methods reported 2,371,826 trials. These do not include a total of 1,181,715 trials, with responses from at least 46,433 subjects, made by the Zenith radio program in the winter of 1937–1938.

The safeguards against error, the methods of procedure, the

statistical analysis, and practically everything relating to the conduct and statistical evaluation of these trials are set forth in the book *Extra Sensory Perception After Sixty Years*, by Joseph A. Greenwood, J. Gaither Pratt, J. B. Rhine, Burke M. Smith, and Charles E. Stuart, all of Duke University. These experiments show conclusively—by methods which cannot be rejected by material science—that man possesses a faculty by which he can gain information from the past to which he has no access through reason and the physical senses; by which he can gain information that no other individual possesses; that is beyond the reach of reason and the physical senses through clairvoyance; and by which he can gain information relative to future events that cannot be known through reason and the physical senses.

Broadly speaking, psychic phenomena fall into two categories. One category embraces the phenomena of gaining information not accessible to reason and the physical senses. Clairvoyance, precognition, telepathy, psychometry and clairaudience are examples of this mental type of phenomena, all of which, whether or not the individual exercising it is under control or in a trance, is embraced within the term extra sensory perception. The other category embraces the phenomena in which physical objects are influenced without the aid of any physical contact with them. Levitation, spirit photographs, trumpet speaking, apports and materializations are instances of the physical type of phenomena which, whether or not the individual exercising it is under control or in a trance, is embraced in the term Extra Physical Power—or to use Duke University terminology, is due to the PK (Psychokinetic) Effect.

Statistical studies at many universities have now conclusively demonstrated that the human soul can not only perceive that which is at a distance and not observable by physical sight, but can gain knowledge of both the past and the future. This seems impossible until it is recognized that consistent with Relativity when velocities exceeding that of light are attained, as they are on the inner plane where the soul of man at all times functions, there is a different order of time, a different order of distance, and a different order of gravitation. Voluminous university experiments reinforce the conclusion of the Zenith Foundation report on its radio tests: "Authentic personal experiences indicate that time is not a factor in telepathic communication. Possession of the ability to visualize in detail events which have not happened, a phenomenon science calls precognition, seems but slightly less rare than telepathy itself."

Future events are seen on the inner plane where the order of time which there obtains makes this possible.

The Zenith Foundation report, which has since been fully confirmed by university experiments and extended by them to include clairvoyance and precognition concludes: "That distance and space are not factors in telepathic communications seem definitely indicated by careful analysis of test returns by geographical divisions."

This is made quite natural by the different order of existence in the realms where the soul functions. According to Relativity, anything moving with 90% the velocity of light shortens to half its length, and at the velocity of light loses all its length. Now as an object cannot have a minus length—that is, a length which is less than nothing—when its velocities are greater than the Boundary-Line energies where it loses all its length, this matter of length, or the accepted order of distance, ceases to have significance.

There are two ways by which information inaccessible to the physical senses and reason can be obtained, both of which derive from laws which logically follow the principle of Relativity. These are through astrology and through extra sensory perception. And in addition to the work done by others, the facts of astrology and the facts of extra sensory perception can be proved by each individual for himself.

The other two orders of facts which form fundamental tenets of The Religion of the Stars are the facts of induced emotion and the facts of directed thinking. Directed thinking steers the inner plane energy to the work to be accomplished, and induced emotion furnishes the energy which is used. Prayers find their answers and people are healed through mental treatments by the application of the principles embraced in these two orders of facts. Physical events are molded and attracted through the power of mind, and the various types of physical psychic phenomena are due to the application of induced emotion and directed thinking.

In spite of the vast amount of careful experiments with materializations and the investigations of hauntings and other physical phenomena by the greatest scientists of earth, it has been possible for certain men skilled in legerdemain to cause most of the public to believe such phenomena have no existence, through offering to produce what appear to be somewhat similar fake phenomena.

But coincident with the experiments conducted at Duke University on extra sensory perception, other experiments were conducted there in great volume on what is called the Psychokinetic Effect. The first report on these exhaustive experiments was made in the March, 1943, issue of *The Journal of Parapsychology*. The experiments conducted were to determine whether by mental power alone hand-thrown and mechanically-released dice could be influenced in a predetermined way. The conclusion of the article starts with this sentence: "At the end of the first PK report, we have to conclude that we know of no better explanation for the result of the tests in dice-throwing herein described than that of the PK hypothesis; i.e., that the subject influenced the fall of the dice without the aid of any recognized physical contact with them."

Each issue of *The Journal of Parapsychology* since has contained further reports and statistical analyses on tests of the Psychokinetic Effect, and the March 1944 number of this journal issued by Duke University Press in the first three paragraphs states:

> The issue of the PK hypothesis can be decided within the scope of a single article. We refer to the paper on the quarter distribution (QD) in this issue.
>
> This abrupt departure from the earlier position is due to the fact that a superior order of evidence has been found which was not known at the time of the first report. In the analysis for the QD there have emerged evidences of Lawfulness in hit patterns throughout so large a portion of the available experimental data that all reasonable doubt of the validity of the PK hypothesis has, we maintain, disappeared, and all counter-hypothesis seem to us manifestly out of the picture.
>
> These statements are, we recognize, very strong, and they must seem to the reader who has not yet read the QD report very bold ones; but they are made with due deliberation and with what we regard as good reason.

Thus it is that not only have the mental types of psychic phenomena been verified by experiments in our universities, but the ability of the soul, or mind, to influence physical phenomena has also now been thoroughly verified by exhaustive experiments in universities. Incontrovertible laboratory proof has been set forth that extra physical power can influence which face of me-chanically-released dice shall appear up. This influence is exerted through a practical application of some of the facts of induced emotion and directed thinking.

Universities have not yet attempted to prove the all-pervading presence of Deific Intelligence, but anyone who develops some degree of extra sensory perception can contact this Intelligence for himself, and get at least some glimpse of the Great Evolutionary Plan. Universities have not yet attempted to demonstrate in the laboratory that the best type of life is that which contributes most to the welfare of all, which is the first of the five fundamental tenets of The Religion of the Stars; but the individual who develops some recognition of his soul through extra sensory perception and a spiritual life can learn this for himself, and can also demonstrate for himself the facts of astrology.

During the first fourteen years of the Pluto Period of the Aquarian Age the universities did demonstrate in an incontro-vertible manner the other three fundamental tenets of The Reli-gion of the Stars. They demonstrated extra sensory perception, induced emotion and directed thinking, even though for the explanation of how these operate the individual must read the Brotherhood of Light lessons.

Pluto's Influence On International Affairs

Pluto rules the invisible world, and as its influence became stronger, the power of this invisible world, and especially of Lower-Pluto entities there residing, became increasingly power-ful. But before appraising the influence of Pluto on political affairs we will get a better perspective if we consider the birthchart of the Aquarian Age and the outstanding progressed aspects which already have formed in it, and the events which have been coin-cident with these progressed aspects.

We should expect the Aquarian Age to begin when the Sun enters Aquarius in the year when the vernal equinox reaches just 30 degrees back of the first of Aries as anciently determined among the stars. This year we have already indicated is 1881. And in 1881 the Sun moved into the sign Aquarius on January 19, at

3h: 48m: 24s P.M., LMT. Washington. The chart here illustrated and erected for this date and time of day is the chart of the Aquarian Age as it affects the United States. For other countries the house positions will be different, and thus the department of life affected by a given progressed aspect will be different; but the same progressed aspects—except those involving the M.C. and Asc.—will take place on practically the same date in every country of the world. And as, regardless of house position, the outstanding events which happen are always characteristic of the planets involved in a progressed aspect at the time, much can be learned of world trends, as well as of the trends within the U.S., from the progressed aspects which form in this chart.

The equinox, which is the most important pointer in this chart, moves backward from Aquarius 29 degrees, 60 minutes, in 1881, at the rate of one degree in 72 years, or 50 seconds in one year. Other than this, the progressed positions are calculated just as they are in the birthchart of an individual. Here we will consider only the Major Progressed Aspects. The Limiting Date—which shows the date during the year when the major progressed positions are their positions as shown in the ephemeris—is September 5, 1880.

1881—Progressed Venus was semi-sextile birthchart Jupiter, ruler of the President (tenth), and in separation (opposition) aspect with birthchart Uranus, the planet of sudden and unexpected events, ruler of the house of death (eighth). James Abraham Garfield, twentieth president of the U.S., was shot and killed.

1882—Progressed Mercury, planet of intellectual interests, was sesqui-square aspect with birthchart Uranus, planet of research and planet of occultism. The Society for Psychical Research was founded.

1886—Progressed Jupiter was inconjunct birthchart Uranus, planet of revolution and agitation; and progressed Mercury, ruler of the house of antagonism (seventh), was in friction (semi-square) aspect with progressed Venus. There were anarchist riots in Chicago.

1888—Progressed Venus, ruler of the house of diplomatic relations (ninth), was in growth (semi-sextile) aspect with birthchart Saturn in the house of our Government (tenth). The first Pan-American Congress met at Washington.

1890—Progressed Mars was in trine aspect with birthchart Neptune. Neptune not only rules corporations, but it rules the watering of stocks and swindles. The Sherman Antitrust Act was passed by Congress.

1893—Mars, ruler of the house of entertainment (fifth), was in luck (trine) aspect with birthchart Uranus, planet of invention. Edison developed moving picture apparatus. Mars, ruler of the house of speculation (fifth), was also in obstacle (square) aspect with birthchart Jupiter, the financial planet, in the house of business (tenth). There was a commercial panic.

1898—Progressed Sun, co-ruler of the house of war (seventh), was in growth (semi-sextile) aspect with progressed Mars, ruler of war. Progressed Mercury, chief ruler of the house of war (seventh), was in obstacle (square) aspect with birthchart Pluto. As the result of war between the U.S. and Spain, Cuba was freed and the U.S. acquired Puerto Rico and the Philippines.

1907—Progressed Sun, ruler of the house of money (second), was square birthchart Pluto, ruler of the house of speculation (fifth). There was a stock panic which started in New York.

1914—Progressed Mars, planet of war, was in prominence (conjunction) aspect with birthchart Sun in the house of war (seventh), and progressed Sun was sextile birthchart Mars. World War I started.

1917—Progressed Sun, co-ruler of the house of war (seventh), made the friction (semi-square) aspect with birthchart Saturn in the house of our Government (tenth), and progressed Mercury made the sextile of birthchart Mercury in the house of war (seventh). The U.S. entered World War I.

1918—Progressed Mercury, ruler of the house of war and partnership (seventh), was trine birthchart Pluto, planet of cooperation. World War I ended and a League of Nations was formed to cooperate in preventing future wars.

1919—Progressed Venus, ruler of the house of diplomatic relations and treaties (ninth), was in prominence (conjunction) aspect with progressed Saturn in the house of Government and the President (tenth). Self-centered Saturn interests persuaded many senators to adopt an isolationist policy, and the Senate refused to ratify the League of Nations Convenant, thus ensuring there would be another World War. President Wilson, on a tour through the country to get the people to insist the League of Nations Covenant be ratified, was stricken with a paralytic stroke which incapacitated him from his usual activities as president.

1929—Progressed Sun, ruler of the house of money (second), was in separation (opposition) aspect with birthchart Moon, ruler of the people (first). A worldwide financial depression started.

This brings us to the Pluto Period which started in 1930. While on its constructive side Pluto works through cooperation, on its adverse side it operates through the coercive tactics characteristic of gangsters.

1931—Mars, planet of war, was in expansion (inconjunct) aspect with progressed Uranus, the sudden planet. Japan suddenly invaded Manchuria, converted it into Manchukuo, and placed that country and its resources under Japanese control.

1933—Progressed Mercury was in separation (opposition) aspect with birthchart Moon, ruler of the people (first), and progressed Sun, ruler of the house of money (second), was semi-sextile progressed Jupiter, co-ruler of the Government (tenth). As a result of the machinery of production and the raw materials for production becoming concentrated in the hands of a few families which were interested primarily in profit, more than ten million people desirous of finding work were out of employment. This so reduced purchasing power that banks all over America began to fail. President Franklin Delano Roosevelt, when he took office in March, temporarily closed all the banks in the country. The Government then made arrangements to insure deposits up to $5,000, and to provide sufficient employment for all that no one need go hungry.

In the meantime, since the Pluto Period started, a peculiarly mediumistic sensitive by the name of Hitler was feeling the impact of the thoughts from the inner plane of a million Germans who had died in World War I. He received his instructions from the invisible world, later having an underground retreat built in the heart of a mountain where he could go and thus commune with those directing his activities. In 1933, under the progressed aspects indicated, he became dictator of Germany. Saturn in the tenth house dominated his own chart, and revenge filled his heart. He taught hate and ruthlessness, spread lies which resulted in the persecution of all who opposed his plans, and was determined, come what might, to fulfill the dreams of world domination held by the warlords of 1914, many of whom, from the other side of life, were now crowding him to action.

1934—Progressed Mercury was still opposition birthchart Moon (the people), and progressed Mars now came to the growth (semi-sextile) aspect with birthchart Venus. As the Western powers, engrossed in their own affairs, had been unwilling to bring heavy sanctions against Japan for acquiring Manchuria through military conquest, Japan now overran and annexed a slice of northern China.

1935—Sun was sextile birthchart Pluto, the gangster planet. During the last of February and the first of March that year, Mars in the sky was moving very slowly, as it was turning retrograde. It was within close orb of opposition to Uranus at this time, and made the perfect square of Pluto. On March 1, suddenly Hitler took over the Saar.

As early as 1922, Benito Mussolini, who had the Sun in Leo and Pluto in the house of war (seventh) in his chart, had established a dictatorship in Italy. With the arrival of the Pluto Period his urge increased to use gangster tactics to expand his fascist empire. As no world organization capable of policing the world had been set up after World War I, the Western powers failed to challenge Japan's expansion through military aggression. Therefore, the Pluto influence increased in power, and Mussolini decided he could acquire new territory in the same manner. As a consequence, in October 1935, after the progressed Sun was well within orb of its sextile with Pluto in the Aquarian Age chart, his troops invaded and conquered Ethiopia. Some economic sanctions were brought against Mussolini by the Western powers, but none of them were willing to go to war with Italy over Ethiopia, as each realized such a move probably would start another world war.

1936—Progressed Sun was sextile birthchart Pluto. As a result of Mussolini's success in using gangster tactics against a weaker nation, dictatorships gained tremendously in power and prestige.

1937—Sun was sextile progressed Pluto; and progressed Venus, ruling the Ascendant (people) in the chart of Japan, was trine progressed Uranus. The Japanese, having assimilated much of northern China, moved their military might to subjugate and take over the whole of China. They met unexpectedly stubborn resistance from the Chinese, and a war started that was to continue and later become an important part of World War II.

1938—Progressed Mars came barely within orb of the expansion (inconjunct) aspect with the Moon, and progressed Mercury made the prominence (conjunction) aspect with birthchart Venus in the house of diplomatic relations (ninth). Stalin, convinced the Nazis of Germany had infiltrated his armed forces and placed his military leaders under their pay so that Germany might conquer Russia, in March conducted a blood purge in which many of these alleged military traitors were executed. About the same time, responding to the racketeer planet Pluto in fine shape, and at a time when Mars was conjunction Uranus in the sky (perfect on March 28), Hitler with his German Nazi troops was ready to make another grab. It was on March 12, 1938 that he invaded Austria.

July 22, 1938, Mars reached the conjunction of Pluto in the sky. Coincident with this Mussolini began to make demands for French territory in the Mediterranean region, and Hitler's Nazis began to stir up trouble in Czechoslovakia. This difficulty resulted in the Munich Pact in September, in which the U.S. was vitally interested. This pact, which was an attempt to appease the dictators, in turn permitted Hitler on October 11, 1938, to grab from Czechoslovakia the Sudetenland.

1939—Progressed Mars was now inconjunct birthchart Moon, and progressed Mercury, chief ruler of the house of war (seventh), was opposition birthchart Uranus. Near the commencement of the astronomical year—the new Sun Cycle which started on March 21, 1939—powerful aspects in various cycle charts were made to Mars, Pluto and Uranus. On March 15, under these astrological influences, Hitler invaded and subjugated Bohemia, Moravia and Slovakia, accomplishing the conquest of Czechoslovakia. On March 28, under the same astrological influences, dictator Franco terminated the Spanish civil war, thus increasing the power of the totalitarian states. On April 1, the Japanese grabbed the French Spratly Islands, only four hours distant from either the Philippines or Singapore. And on April 6, Mussolini invaded and conquered Albania.

It was plain to all that the dictators were started on the road to domination of the whole world. Therefore, when at the beginning of September, Germany commenced the invasion of Poland, both Britain and France gave her an ultimatum to cease. This ultimatum expired on September 3, on which date England and France officially entered what became World War II.

1940—Mars was semi-square birthchart Mars, progressed Mercury was opposition birthchart Uranus, and progressed

Venus was trine birthchart Uranus, planet of the unusual. France and the Low Countries were overrun in May and conquered by Germany. September 27 there was formed the Berlin-Rome-Tokyo Axis, an agreement in which, except for Russia, any country at war with Germany, Italy or Japan automatically was also at war with the other two Axis nations. The United States traded obsolete destroyers to Britain for naval bases, a selective service act was passed to acquire soldiers, and Franklin Delano Roosevelt shattered a precedent by being elected for a third term as president.

1941—Progressed Venus, ruling the house of treaties (ninth), was conjunction progressed Neptune, ruler of Japan. Progressed Venus was trine birthchart Uranus. Progressed Mercury was opposition birthchart Uranus, trine progressed Venus, and trine progressed Neptune, planet of idealism. On June 22 Germany suddenly and unexpectedly (Uranus) invaded and made war on Russia. To assist the nations resisting aggression from the totalitarian powers, the U.S. instituted a Lend-Lease program by which these nations could acquire supplies for the conduct of the war.

Late in 1940 The Church of Light published its brochure on the Nine-Point Plan for The New Civilization, and on January 5, 1941, started regular Crusade Talks each month advocating this Nine-Point Plan. These monthly talks spread to many cities throughout the United States and continue. At this writing such meetings are held regularly in approximately 50 different cities. Four of these nine points then, and now, advocated were that all the people of the world should have Freedom from Want, Freedom from Fear, Freedom of Expression, and Freedom of Worship.

In August 1941, Franklin Delano Roosevelt, President of the U.S., and Winston Churchill, Prime Minister of England, met in the Atlantic Ocean and agreed on certain principles which were to govern the postwar world. This agreement, which at the time was not placed in writing, and which embraced practically the same four freedoms The Church of Light had been advocating for a year in its Nine-Point Plan, was called the Atlantic Charter. The principles of the Atlantic Charter were agreed to in writing by 26 of the United Nations in January, 1942.

On December 7, 1941, Japan made a sneak attack on Pearl Harbor, sinking many U.S. naval vessels in the Hawaiian harbor, thus badly crippling the U.S. Pacific Fleet, and commencing war on the United States. Immediately both its Axis partners, Germany and Italy, also declared war on the U.S.

1942—Progressed Mercury was opposition birthchart Uranus and sextile progressed Neptune. Through military conquests, Japan rapidly expanded her empire to vast proportions, conquering the Philippines, taking Singapore, Burma, the Dutch East Indies, New Guinea, and being stopped just short of invading Australia.

1944—Progressed Sun, co-ruler of the house of war (seventh), was square birthchart Mars, and progressed Mars was sextile birthchart Saturn in the house of Government (tenth). U.S. forces successfully invaded Africa early in 1943 and Italy later in the year, and successfully invaded France in 1944. Russian troops rolled the Nazis back on the eastern front, while British and American forces hit them from the west. One after another the countries that had been invaded by the Nazis were liberated. The Japanese also were made to yield much of their conquered territory, and cities in Japan were bombed. U.S. forces successfully landed in the Philippines.

1945—Mercury at 12° Pisces 51′, and thus in opposition with birthchart Uranus, sextile progressed Neptune, and semi-sextile birthchart Jupiter, will turn direct in motion. Progressed Uranus will be sesqui-square birthchart Mercury; and progressed Jupiter will be in agitation (sesqui-square) aspect with progressed Uranus, sextile birthchart Pluto, and square birthchart Mercury. All seven of these aspects will last for a number of years.

These are the dominant progressed aspects until 1949, when progressed Mars comes to the square of birthchart Pluto, moving on to the square of progressed Pluto and the sextile of progressed Jupiter in 1950. In 1949 progressed Venus comes within orb of trine birthchart Moon, making the perfect aspect in 1950. The last of 1950 also shows Mercury moving more than one degree past the perfect opposition of birthchart Uranus. After 1950 the progressed aspects in the chart for the Aquarian Age are not so significant for some years.

The significance of the progressed aspects following 1944 in this chart can only be recognized in connection with the Neptune Cycle which commenced March 7, 1944, 10:57 a.m. LMT, Washington, D.C. A planet's cycle starts when it crosses the celestial equator from south to north declination. Those things which the planet rules are strongly accentuated in the minds and actions of men near the commencement of its cycle. Neptune rules both involuntary servitude and the ideals which free man from bondage. Before the present one, the last Neptune cycles were in 1863. They brought a surge of Neptune idealism which resulted in the emancipation of the Negroes in America. The present Neptune cycle, which will last well into the twenty-first century, marks a surge of Neptune idealism demanding the emancipation of all the people of the world.

It demands that there shall be equal economic opportunities, equal political opportunities, equal educational opportunities, and equal opportunities to use recreational, health and other public services for all the people on the globe. It demands that there shall be Freedom from Want, Freedom from Fear, Freedom of Expression, and Freedom of Worship in every country of the world. These opportunities and these freedoms are on the way. They are mankind's natural heritage from the Aquarian Age. They are sure to arrive. The only question is, how soon?

It is certain they will not arrive without a struggle. And that is the significance of progressed Mercury opposition Uranus and sextile Neptune in the Aquarian Age chart exerting its influence from 1945 to 1950. And it is the significance also of progressed Mars square Pluto in the Aquarian Age chart in 1949 and 1950. These heavy aspects to all three upper octave planets show that a mighty effort will be made to free the world from the economic, political and intellectual tyranny which was characteristic of the Age of Pisces. And they show also that selfish interests will put up a tremendous fight to prevent the realization of these ideals.

It is not to be expected that these freedoms and opportunities will be realized by 1950. All that can be hoped for is that by that time political and diplomatic machinery will be set up which will ensure fairly rapid progress toward them. And if political and diplomatic machinery are not set up which will convince people that these freedoms and opportunities are on the way, World War III is inevitable.

However long it takes, and no matter how many disastrous world wars it takes, the people of the world will not be denied these opportunities and these freedoms long after the equinox has become fully polarized in the Aquarian Age. Furthermore, although more time will be required to reach so many people with their benefits, the people of the Aquarian Age are going to acquire and utilize the facts of astrology, the facts of extra sensory perception, the facts of induced emotion and the facts of directed thinking.

For many years we have had the opportunity to watch those with a thorough knowledge of astrology who have applied directed thinking and induced emotion based on that knowledge. We have watched the development of children who have been trained in a manner specifically designed to develop into abilities the natural aptitudes shown in their charts of birth, and we have observed the events which came into the lives of adults who employed the indicated precautionary actions for the progressed aspects which were operative in their charts. The result of these observations is the conviction that through standard astrology and the application of induced emotion and directed thinking the effectiveness and the happiness of human life can be doubled.

In the word effectiveness, I include material success, intellectual development and spiritual progress. And the world will not move far into the Aquarian Age before most people, through applying induced emotion and directed thinking as advised by astrological knowledge, will greatly increase their effectiveness.

They also will be taught more and more about the principles on which the universe is run. They will understand, not merely that they have a soul, but of what it consists, how it arrived at its present state of development, and about the opportunities for its progress in the realms of the future. And when they thus grasp the trend of the Cosmic Plan they will perceive how shortsighted it is for individuals and nations greedily to promote what they think are their own interests at the expense of less fortunate individuals or less powerful nations.

No longer will people be blinded either by the narrow doctrines of academic materialists or by the doctrines of intolerant orthodox religion. So long as man believes death ends all, a great wall shuts off his vision, and he can perceive nothing but matter. And so long as he believes in an after-death life where the individual lives without progress in heaven or blisters without hope in hell, his mind is so completely focused on this hallucination that nothing else can be perceived.

But soon the energies of the Aquarian Age will free man's mind from such slavery, and he will either use his own extra sensory perception to investigate Nature, or will accept the findings of others who have used extra sensory perception to investigate other realms of life. His conception of Nature will broaden, and he will understand that there are inner planes of existence where intelligences dwell, and that there he will dwell after physical dissolution. And he will perceive that on these inner planes he will have opportunity for development and progress, and that he is being educated now, and will be educated on the inner planes in the future, to perform a significant function in the universal scheme. That will bring him to the conviction that as all people in the world also are undergoing their education to fill a niche in the cosmic scheme of the future, they should have as many opportunities in human life as possible. He will believe that all people should have the four freedoms because, among other things, this will facilitate their education; and the welfare of the whole depends upon their education.

The Aquarian Age, at not too distant a date, will thus awaken people to a true general conception of how the universe is managed, and they will perceive that the world also should be run, not upon the principle of cut-throat competition and war, but upon the principle of specialization of parts, division of labor and complete cooperation between the parts. Between the time this section on Pluto's Influence on International Affairs is being written (1944) and the end of 1950 there will be opportunity for the world to set up the political and diplomatic machinery through which mankind will move rapidly toward the ideals here set forth. But one characteristic of the influence of Pluto when afflicted is that as soon as one group is formed to carry out some worthwhile purpose, another group springs up drastically to oppose and try to block the effort of the worthy group. Therefore, during the years of adjustment, especially until the end of 1950, we may expect those with whose special privileges widespread knowledge and the four freedoms would interfere to make a bitter stand against their realization.

The leaders of intolerant religious groups realize that to maintain their special privilege their followers must keep convinced that they alone should be permitted to interpret the will of Deity. Their followers must look up to them as superior to ordinary human beings. And not only do the leaders of these intolerant religious groups try to suppress the teachings of astrology and extra sensory perception, which would reveal their pretenses to be without foundation, but they struggle for a political power that will enable them eventually to suppress all religions but their own.

In addition to intolerant religious authorities there are also equally intolerant academic individuals. These atheistic materialists stand before the world as the final authority. Their special privilege is not that of wealth, but that of prestige. Whatever they say is true must not be disputed. If they say there is no inner plane, no one must produce proof that life survives after physical dissolution on such a plane. If they say the planets cannot influence people, no one must be permitted to present statistical studies proving they actually do influence human life. And these atheistic materialists will stop at nothing to discredit any who produce proof they are wrong. For to show them in error is to destroy their special privilege.

Even without the new energies which soon will be available for human use, which are discussed in Chapter 10, right now with proper division of labor every person in the world could occupy his energies in producing something that either sustains life or makes life richer. Hit or miss methods, to be sure, may make an unusable surplus of some products; but for what was man given brains if not to ensure he would use his energies not in producing vast quantities of one thing at the expense of producing other things of which he has greater need?

Raw materials are available, machinery is available, and the manpower and skill are available at this moment—as production for World War II has amply demonstrated—to enable every person in the world to be free from want. And a correct appraisal of God's Great Plan shows that all the people of the world should thus have freedom from want. But the steps necessary to obtain such a desirable condition would deprive some of the means of profiteering, and others of their practice of exploiting backward peoples. Therefore those who thus would be deprived of their special privileges resort to many cunning devices, including the spreading of lies, to prevent people from learning the facts which would lead to such economic freedom.

The Aquarian Age certainly will bring man the four freedoms, and it certainly will bring him knowledge of the facts of astrology, knowledge of the facts of extra sensory perception, knowledge of the facts of induced emotion, and knowledge of the facts of directed thinking. In due time it will usher in The New Civilization. But between now and the end of 1950 special privilege will do all in its power to discredit and suppress astrology and extra sensory perception, and all in its power to thwart the realization of the four freedoms. But in spite of that opposition, at least some progress will be made, with the probabilities favorable that a foundation will be laid for future progress.

But should special privilege succeed, by any foul chance, in thwarting the move toward The New Civilization at that time, there will be another and more destructive world war. For whatever it takes in suffering to educate mankind to it, the Aquarian Age will eliminate special privilege and devise a world organization built on the plan of division of labor, specialization of parts and the efficient cooperation of those parts.

The advance toward this New Civilization will be taken one step at a time. And even the first step may take years of struggle. Let no one think that at the end of World War II world struggle shortly will cease. But we can hope that by the end of 1950 the first step will have been completed. That first step, which true religion will do all in its power to foster, and special privilege will do all in its power to hinder, is the realization, not merely in America, but by all the peoples of the globe, of the statement made in The Declaration of Independence, that all men are created equal (with equal right to have the opportunity to develop the natural potentialities indicated in their planetary chart of birth), and that all men have a right to be free.

Chapter 9

The Astrological Quantum of Action

here are two avenues through which information not accessible to the physical senses and reason may be gained. One is the avenue of astrology. The other is the avenue of extra sensory perception. All methods of divination depend upon the exercise of extra sensory perception, which is the ability of the soul to gain information through its inner plane activities and to impress that information on objective consciousness in a recognizable form. Due to velocities on the inner plane being greater than that of light, where time stands still and objects lose all their length, the soul functioning on the inner plane readily can acquire information, including past, present and future, quite inaccessible to reason and the physical senses. It is this ability that gives divination in any of its forms its value.

While extra sensory perception plays an important part in horary astrology, and may be used in reading any chart, the correct reading of a birthchart and progressed aspects does not require the use of extra sensory perception. On the contrary, scientific astrology, through plotting the heavenly bodies, endeavors to appraise the power of inner plane energies radiated by the planets, modified by the signs as sounding boards and given harmonious or discordant trends by the aspects, to influence not merely human life, but all earthly affairs. The houses through which the energies are received indicate the department of life or world affairs thus affected.

If we could turn on extra sensory perception at will, it would no doubt outrank astrology in its usefulness. But in our present state of knowledge no one seems able to do this. And even in its use—unless it employs astrology on the inner plane—it seldom is able to time events. Astrology, on the other hand, times events within well-defined periods, but fails to give the precision of detail often obtained through the use of extra sensory perception.

Within limits which have largely been determined through statistical studies, it can be ascertained from his birthchart what the outstanding traits of character of an individual are, whether he will be fortunate or unfortunate relative to each of the 12 departments of his life, the type of events he will experience, and about when they will arrive. But in addition to the factors indicated by astrology, conditioning by environment, as explained in detail in *When and What Events Will Happen*, and the environmental conditions by which he is surrounded at a particular time, as explained in detail in *Progressed Aspects of Standard Astrology*, also influence both the individual's character and the events which come into his life.

Thus astrologers are in the same position in determining what will occur in the life of a given individual as are the physical scientists in determining where a physical object will be at a given time. By applying Einstein's Special Theory of Relativity, physical scientists can predict, from the momentum, velocity, direction of movement, and other physical conditions and a proper system of coordinates, the behavior of physical objects larger than molecular proportions. They can determine in advance where a planet will be in its orbit, how much a rifle ball will be deflected by wind and gravitation in a measured distance, how long it will take an airplane traveling at a definite speed to cross the Atlantic. But with particles of molecular size and smaller they have no ability to make such definite predictions. Einstein admits that so far the precise laws governing the behavior of particles have baffled him, and until they are ascertained there can be no Unified Field Theory such as he had hoped to formulate.

Quite a number of years ago, Plank discovered that the radiation of energy is not a uniformly continuous process, but occurs in impulses containing not less than a definite amount of energy in each impulse. In other words, as atoms once were considered to be particles of matter which could not be subdivided further, so all energy seems to manifest in bundles which cannot be subdivided by any known means into smaller units of energy. The energy in a light beam seems to be concentrated in bundles, called photons, which have properties similar to those of particles. Yet even though a photon—the smallest unit of light—carries energy and momentum, it differs from a particle in that its rest mass is zero. That which has no rest mass is immaterial, and it is because light is thus immaterial that physicists believe it has in space a fixed velocity.

Thus, not only matter but energy also is supposed by physicists to be composed of units, or building bricks, which themselves are not divisible. The negative energy moving through a wire from lower to higher potential (called electricity) is constructed of grains, called electrons, which are the elementary, or smallest, quanta of electricity. These same electrons enter into and form the outer envelope of each atom of matter. Therefore, electrons are also elementary quanta of matter; and neither electricity nor matter can be decreased in smaller "jumps" than that represented by an electron.

Not only radio waves and visible light waves are composed of photons, but X-rays and gamma rays. Yet cosmic rays, which possess far greater energy and penetrating power in their primary state, are not composed of photons, but of particles. This brings in another discovery in addition to that of both energy radiation and particle radiation being possible only discontinuously in terms of elementary quanta; the discovery that not only energy, but particles of matter also, are guided in their motion by waves. It was Davisson, Gerner, and G. P. Thompson who confirmed de Broglie's theory of the wave properties of material particles, and Schrodinger who proved that such material particles are guided in their motion in the same way that light is guided. But whether the radiation is electromagnetic in nature—which includes visible light—or particled, "The energy emitted divided by the frequency of the radiations is always equal to a certain unit of 'action,' which we call the Quantum of Action."

Furthermore, light, for instance, exhibits properties which can only be explained by assuming it to be a wave, and other properties which can only be explained by assuming it to be corpuscular. For a discussion of these apparent contradictions the reader is referred to *The Evolution of Physics* (1938) by Albert Einstein and Leopold Infeld. From this book I quote the last paragraph of the summary on Quanta:

> Is light a wave or a shower of photons? Is a beam of electrons a
> shower of elementary particles or a wave? These fundamental

questions are forced upon physics by experiment. In seeking to
answer them we have to abandon the description of atomic events
as happening in space and time, we have to retreat still further from
the old mechanical view. Quantum physics formulates laws governing crowds and not individuals. Not properties but probabilities are described, not laws disclosing the future of systems are
formulated, but laws governing the changes in time of the probabilities and relating to great congregations of individuals.

This brings us to the Principle of Indeterminancy, which was
first discovered by Heisenberg and Bohr, and now has become an
essential portion of modern physics. To indicate in a few paragraphs its most important implications, I will quote from physicists of outstanding accomplishment:

> The electron has a certain degree of 'freedom,' and many physicists
> believe that if there is anything at all that determines the position and
> motion of the electron within the limits set by the quantum of action,
> that something may well be entirely outside the domain of physics.

I believe this is true, that particles on the boundary line of
velocities between those of the physical world and those of the
astral world are influenced by both realms. Such particles other
than within the boundaries of what the physicist calls the quantum have their position determined by physical environment.
Therefore, from the physical conditions alone their positions can
be predicted to be somewhere within these boundaries. But inside
the boundaries of this quantum of action, their position is not
determined by physical forces or external environment, but by
astrological and other astral forces.

So also, by the method of statistical analysis employed in the
three books, *How To Select A Vocation*, *When and What Events Will
Happen*, and *Body Disease and Its Stellar Treatment*, from the astrological positions alone it can be predicted that an individual will
have characteristics and aptitudes of a certain type, and that he
will have thoughts of a certain type and experience events of a
certain type during a given period of his life. But inside the
boundaries of this astrological quantum of action the specific
channels through which the indicated characteristics will express,
and the specific thoughts and specific events which he will experience during a certain period, are not indicated by astrology, but

are determined by the manner in which he has been conditioned by past events, and by the environment in which, during the period, he finds himself.

> To quote further relative to the quantum of action of physics: The product of these uncertainties can never be smaller than the quantum of action. The pilot waves can thus determine the position of an electron at a future time within a certain degree of probability. We may say that the electron is always within the pilot wave, but where it is and how it is moving within the wave is not determined by any physical law at all.

And neither is the specific occupation followed by an individual, nor the specific event which comes into his life, indicated by astrology. But the type of occupation, and the type of event, are thus indicated. Yet within the type, within the astrological quantum of action, there are alternative occupations, and alternative events.

We may define the birthchart quantum of action to lie within boundaries such as afford experiences characteristic of the prominence and aspects of the planets, and such as are characteristic of the planetary type of activity and the harmony or discord of the houses, as mapped by the birthchart.

These boundaries can only be so narrow as experiences in lower life forms provide scope for the indicated planetary and house activity. In lower forms of life, as set forth in *How To Select A Vocation*, there are opportunities to build into the soul thought elements of each of the ten families mapped in the birthchart by the ten planets, opportunities to build them into the soul relative to any department of life such as mapped by a house in the birthchart, and opportunities to build them either harmoniously or discordantly, as mapped by the aspects, into thought compounds with other thought elements mapped by other planets.

But there are not opportunities below human existence for experiences with mathematics, with foreign languages, with automobiles, with serving table in a cafe, with moving pictures, with photography, with moral or immoral conduct, or with any number of specialized vocations and activities in which man engages. These special trends are all products of the conditioning, or educating, effects of the earlier environment, providing easier facilities for the planetary energies and house activities to express in some specialized conditions and events and offering resistance to other specialized conditions and events—that is, to alternate conditions and events—through which the same birthchart energies can express without going outside of the astrological quantum of action.

The progressed astrological quantum of action lies within boundaries such as afford conditions or an event which bears the characteristics of one or more of the planets forming the progressed aspect, and which belongs to the department of life ruled by one of the houses governed by the planets making the progressed aspect.

Usually the importance of the event to the individual, and its tendency to be fortunate or unfortunate, are also indicated by the progressed aspect; but as these are so powerfully subject to modification through intelligent conditioning and selection of environment, they, as well as the specific kind of event, lie within the astrological quantum of action of the individual who understands astrology and makes a definite effort based upon that knowledge.

Our *Case History Studies of Environment and Conditioning as Affecting Events Attracted by Identical Progressed Aspects to Those Possessing Practically Identical Birthcharts* have demonstrated that conditioning alone can change the specific event, its importance, its harmony or discord, and to which of several alternate houses ruled by the aspecting planets it relates. And they have demonstrated that even when the conditioning previously has been similar, that two widely different environments may cause the specific event, its importance, its harmony or discord, and to which of several alternate houses ruled by the aspecting planets it relates, to be different.

Even as there is a physical quantum of action, so also is there an astrological quantum of action. The boundaries of the astrological quantum of action are ascertained by the statistically determined birthchart constants and progressed constants. The value of knowing the astrological quantum of action of a character trait or an event lies in the power this knowledge gives to take proper Precautionary Actions which will ensure the character trait expressed or the event attracted will be specifically the most beneficial one of the various alternates within the astrological quantum of action.

The Coming Civilization

ature has clearly indicated the direction in which civilization is moving. Following the broad pattern taken in the evolution of life forms in general, it is moving in the direction of a world organism in which certain groups of people will perform the function of one organ in the human body, and other groups of people each will perform the functions of other organs in the human body, and all will be working together for the benefit of the whole.

Nations possessing certain natural aptitudes and raw materials will use these for the benefit of all the people of the world, and nations possessing other natural aptitudes and raw materials will use these for the benefit of all the people of the world. And people within a nation will cease their hit-or-miss method of selecting a vocation. Instead they will be specially educated from early years to enable them to develop to the highest degree of efficiency, and use for the benefit of all the people in the world, the natural aptitudes shown by their planetary charts of birth.

Even with energies which already have been brought under control, and present technical skill, present machinery, present raw material, and present manpower, a world thus organized would free every man, woman and child from want. But already on the horizon there are both new energies of incalculable power, and new controls of infinite delicacy, which presently will be used for the benefit of mankind.

People are merely beginning to understand how electronics may be employed to direct and control more ponderous energies. But the time will come when they will be used not merely to manipulate various types of physical power, but also freely to communicate between those who have lost their physical bodies through so-called death, and those still residing on the physical plane. Electronics, in due time, will make conversation, by purely mechanical means, between those on the spirit side of life with those on the earth side of life, as common and as easy as it is now common and easy for those in different cities to converse with each other over the telephone.

Relative to the effect the new energies now on the horizon will be likely to have, history indicates that wherever the arts, science, literature, philosophy, and even religion have shown commendable development, there have been men with leisure to develop them, a leisure made possible through utilizing energies other than their own. Even Christianity made slight progress until espoused by the accumulated wealth and surplus force of Rome. Historians believe that Rome, Egypt, Babylon and Greece advanced to the civilizations for which they are noted because each at times had available for every free man the energy of one human slave plus another slave's energy from mechanical and animal sources.

Without citing still earlier cultures built on the average freeman having at his command the energy of one slave, or the development of feudalism and the commencement of our own era, both made possible by an increasing energy surplus, a census of 1869 informs us that after the abolition of slavery the combined power of draft animals and machines gave to each man, woman and child in the United States an additional energy the equivalent of 12 slaves. That is, the energy available for productive purposes was six times as great as that of the ancient civilizations at their height.

Yet the 1930 census, at the commencement of the Pluto Period, indicates at that time the average person in the United States had available, in the form of automobiles, locomotives, manufacturing plants, power stations, horses, etc., the equivalent of 177 slaves. Let us therefore, with a view to possible future changes when the new powers now on the horizon are developed, scan one or two of the more important modifications this increase of energy has already brought to our civilization.

Primitive man, no doubt, was more or less nomadic, and a hunter. But with the development of agriculture, life became more secure, and many institutions were developed which have persisted almost to our day. The hunter needed strength, agility, bravery and cunning; but with the more settled routine of the quiet farm, thrift and industriousness became qualities of greater need; the woman became more valuable than heretofore, because of the innumerable tasks she could perform.

Likewise, because children could be compelled to work for their keep, and their labor capitalized, large families were encouraged. Even with the beginning of industrial pursuits, because these were still carried out in the home largely by women and children, there continued to be taught the doctrine that women should be meek, should bear as many children as possible, should dress and act in a manner more constrained than men, and that their place was exclusively in the home.

This time-honored conception of the sheltered and subservient position of woman, and the view that any attempt to limit the number of children to the physical strength of the mother and the possibility of their adequate support was a cardinal sin, persisted century after century, until new energy supplies made radical changes in family life imperative.

The development of machinery drove industrial activity from the country and home to the city, the office and the factory. The demand for female workers made them economically independent, but it also made impractical the old order of home life. Children, because their labor no longer could be capitalized, and because of the loss of work to the mother while bearing and caring for them, became a luxury. Under the agricultural regime the man of 18 to 21 had sufficient knowledge to support himself, and the addition of a wife and numerous children were aids to the acquisition of a competence. But the skill now required for a young man to handle the intricate machines, or the business responsibility of industry, with sufficient adequacy to support a wife in the standards to which she has become accustomed in the parental home is seldom reached before thirty.

In the United States, 1930—the commencement of the Pluto Period—found eleven million women gainfully employed. Doing the same work as men, they have tended to adopt the same dress as men, to wear their hair like men, to smoke and drink and swear as their male companions do, and to ask for a single standard in moral conduct. Men and women now reach physical maturity and are beset with the same biological urges as previously; yet marriage of necessity is delayed an extra ten years. Meantime, the movies, the radio and cheap magazines are financially successful in proportion as they stimulate amorous desires. Children are a luxury, marriage is postponed and increasingly avoided, unconventional attachments flourish, and the home frequently is but a few cells in the honeycomb of some concrete structure; all due to the development of energies that make of this a machine age. It is not to criticize this state of affairs, which is but the natural outcome of compelling environmental forces, that this is mentioned; but to point out the cause, and to indicate it is but a transitory level in far greater changes now at hand.

There can be no doubt, in spite of crime-wave and gang warfare, also made possible and encouraged by easily-accessible energy supplies, as well as by the violation of the fundamentals of psychology, that present day advantages are more numerous than its drawbacks. Under such rapid change it is difficult to determine what is wrong and what for the best. The shorter hours of labor give more opportunity for personal development. The movie, the newspaper, the radio and the automobile are each vast engines of education. People live fuller lives now than ever before. But new energies have brought with them a change in the setup of civilization. And still other energies which can be used to build an environment of human happiness also can construct engines of terrible destruction to enslave the people and make more horrible the conduct of war. Although they have not as yet been utilized, such other energies are known to exist.

In addition to the astrological energies which so profoundly affect human life, and new energies already known, there may be still others at present unrecognized by science. This presumption is based upon the fact that the most potent energies now known were not discovered until 1925, yet these cosmic rays afford energies a thousandfold greater than are available from any other source. They afford energies surely as high as 6 billion electron volts, and probably higher than 10 billion electron volts. By way of comparison, the "light bullets" (photons) emitted from an electric lamp represent energies of about 2 electron volts; X-rays may develop from 20 thousand to 100 thousand electron volts; and gamma rays from radium about 2½ million electron volts. The most probable source of new power, however, is the binding energy of the atom.

Early in 1939 the artificial fission of uranium was discovered.

Painstaking work revealed that it was not the common form of uranium which was split into two other elements, but the isotope U235. Large deposits of Uranium are found in Germany, Canada, the Belgian Congo and Colorado. U235 occurs in the ore in about the proportion of 1 part to 139 parts of the common U238.

On the fifth of May, 1940, Dr. Alfred O. C. Nier, of the University of Minnesota, announced a method, since corroborated in other universities, of isolating U235. And as this is written scientists the world over are working on the problem of extracting it from uranium ores in commercial quantities.

When neutrons are slowed down by passing through hydrogenous matter such as water and paraffin, these slow neutrons are readily captured by the nucleus of atoms. This results in the formation of an isotope which is heavier than the stable form. The instability then may result in the emission of gamma rays or the emission of an electron. But in the case of U235, instead of gaining stability through the ordinary processes of radioactivity, the capture of a slow neutron by the nucleus results in the uranium atom, which has 92 protons, splitting into the atoms of two other elements, barium, having 56 protons, and krypton, having 36 protons.

Such a complete fission of an atom is something quite new to science. Yet associated with it are two other amazing features. One is that in the splitting, neutrons are released to bombard other nuclei, so that a chain reaction results. Once the process is started in a given mass of U235 it continues until all is broken into the two mentioned elements. The other is that in the process matter is converted into energy; that is, atomic binding energy is released due to the disparity between the weights of the separated groups of particles and the weight of the nucleus just previous to breaking up after capturing a neutron.

Naturally radioactive elements may produce 14 million electron volt alpha particles, but fission of U235 produces 100 million electron volt barium particles. Dr. Nier estimates that one pound of U235 would generate as much force as the combustion of 2 million pounds of coal, and that its explosive energy is equivalent to that of 20 million pounds of high explosives.

Others have pointed out that a small amount, a pound or two, if its energy could be completely utilized, would drive an oceanliner for months. They have asserted that all that would be required to keep releasing its energies would be to place it in water. The water would be converted into steam, and the steam could be used to run turbines. When the water was used up the process would stop, and start up again only when new water was added.

All of which sounds entirely too easy and simple. There are difficult problems awaiting those who attempt to harness U235. Nevertheless the energy is there, and on a small scale even at present can be released. Furthermore, the binding energy released in this fission is only a small fraction of the total energy which would develop if one unit of atomic weight could be converted into energy. Such conversion, if possible, would yield about a billion electron volts.

It was a method to release and use this energy within the atom that Hitler's scientists were so feverishly trying to discover during World War II; and had they been successful before the end of the war (as this is written World War II is still in progress and Germany as yet undefeated) the whole world would come under the cruel heel of Nazi tyranny.

And this thought emphasizes the most significant factor of all relative to the coming civilization. That factor is not whether new energies of tremendous power are going to be discovered—for such discoveries are on the way—but whether the new energies made available will be used by special privilege to exploit the masses and keep them subservient, or will be used to benefit the people as a whole. Already I have indicated that in 1930 the energy of 177 slave power was available for the use of the average man. But did that additional energy bring freedom from want? It certainly did not; because it became concentrated in the hands of a few families. It became the tool of special privilege. People could neither acquire the raw materials nor the machines of production; for these were owned by those who were interested, not in supplying people with the things the machines could produce from the raw materials, but with the profit they could make. As a consequence, by 1933 there were ten million unemployed in the U.S., and a year or two later over fourteen million people in the U.S. desiring employment who could not get it.

We have seen the changes wrought when man had at his command energies the equivalent of 177 slaves. What changes will be induced when, as soon will be the case, the average individual has at his command 1,000 slave-power? With the sensitive controls the science of electronics gives over such tremendous energies, we cannot envision the facilities man will be able to utilize. But we may be sure that, as in the past, so in the future, there will be those who will try to use these energies to benefit themselves at the expense of the rest of mankind.

Against such brutal, selfish men mankind has but one protection: to increase in knowledge and spirituality. Increase in spirituality increases the desire that all shall prosper, and motivates work to that end. Increase in knowledge enables these desires to be implemented by effective methods of thwarting those who would exploit and oppress others, and by methods of action by which the ideals may be made into realities. Increased spirituality united to increased knowledge alone will abolish special privilege and give to all the people of the world Freedom from Want, Freedom from Fear, Freedom of Expression and Freedom of Worship.

Midsummer Sunrise and the Forgotten Rites of Stonehenge

n the County of Wiltshire, England, still may be seen the ruins of what is probably the most perfect example of its kind of an ancient temple of the Religion of the Stars.

Stonehenge has been reconstructed as a model; and the archaeologists are able to furnish a detailed description of its original appearance and structure. Their opinion is that it was built about four thousand years ago.

The history of the region goes back about half that far—only to the time of the Roman conquest. At this much later date, Roman history records that the Druid priests taught many things about the size and dimensions of the heavens and the various motions of the stars; that they believed the soul of man had previously occupied lower forms of life; and that after death man lives, much as he lives on earth, in some superior region.

With this account of the beliefs of those still inhabiting the vicinity at the time of the Roman invasion, let us read Stonehenge in terms of its own language, the language of universal symbolism. The long avenue of stones leading from the northeast indicates the path of evolution leading through lower forms of life up to the state of human birth. The direction of approach is from the northeast, because it is from the northeast that the soul is born; that is, the house of birth, the first house of a birth chart, is in the northeast part of the map.

The outside of this temple consists of a circular earthwork three hundred feel in diameter. Because the constellations surrounding the zodiac, and picturing its influence, are composed of an infinite number of stars, such a mound, not distinguished by well-marked divisions, well represents the surrounding starry firmaments.

Immediately within this earthwork originally was a circle of small "foreign stones," the foundations of which only now remain. These "foreign stones" represent the influence of the zodiac and its divisions.

Then, interior to these, comes a complete ring of hewn stones with lintels mortised to their tops, making a series of doorways. These doorways, extending completely around the circle, are not made of "foreign stones," because the houses of a birth chart are not dependent upon stellar influences, but upon the position on the earth where such influences fall. Inside this ring of stone doorways is another ring of "foreign stones," indicating the motion of the planets in their orbits.

Within these is a horseshoe of five dolmens. The number five is the symbol of man, and was so considered in all the ancient schools. A dolmen, consisting of two upright stones with a horizontal stone on top, is a doorway; the horizontal stone conveys the idea of a higher plane. The five dolmens signify the belief that man passes through the doorway of physical dissolution to continue life and effort in a higher realm.

Within the five dolmens is a horseshoe of "foreign stones." The horseshoe form is the symbol of the feminine in nature, even as the single upright stone is the symbol of the masculine. The crescent is also the symbol of the Moon. Within the curve of this horseshoe is a flat, horizontal slab of stone serving as an altar.

In this temple many different ceremonies were performed, but only one will be mentioned here. The neophyte to be initiated, standing on this slab of stone within the horseshoe at sunrise on the day of the summer solstice, portrayed the age-old mystery of the immaculate conception. In the center of the avenue of approach, and so located that the rising Sun on the longest day of the year sheds its rays directly over it into the horseshoe and upon the altar, is a large, unworked, upright stone, representing the Sun and the masculine in nature.

In nature there is a constructive principle and a destructive principle. Light is the universal symbol of the constructive attribute, while darkness is representative of that which is destructive. At the time of the summer solstice the day is longest, the Sun highest in the heavens. Symbolically, the power of light then reaches its maximum. The neophyte, standing on the altar as the rising Sun that day sheds its light over the Sun stone, represents the soul within the womb of matter, reunited to its divine source by a spiritual ray.

The avenue and its stones indicate the steps he has taken to reach his present illumination. His position reveals his knowledge that physical life is merely a period of gestation, from which he will be born into the life of a more glorious existence. He is surrounded by symbols that represent the mundane houses, the zodiac and the planets, indicating that he recognizes their influence both upon his life here and upon his life on the higher plane, signified by the dolmens.

The "foreign stones" which represent the influence of the zodiac, the circling planets and the crescent Moon, have not been quarried, like the other stones, in the near vicinity; but to represent their influence as coming from afar, have been brought from some distant place.

The neophyte, with the light of the rising Sun shining upon him this longest day of the year, has come into a realization of the meaning of life; that life below is a preparatory school in which the soul is trained according to the function it is to perform in the universal organization. His soul entered matter to gain this training, and now, as indicated by the rays of the rising Sun reaching him, it is once more consciously united to its ego, to the sun of its divine source.

Now and hereafter, astrological forces will play their part. But having arrived at the state of true illumination, he is no longer a neophyte, for he is conscious of his cosmic work.

C. C. Zain

21 COURSE STUDY PROGRAM
ON THE
HERMETIC SCIENCES

Astrology ❖ Alchemy ❖ Magic

VOL	TITLE	PRICE
1	Laws of Occultism	$11.95
2	Astrological Signatures	13.95
3	Spiritual Alchemy	11.95
4	Ancient Masonry	13.95
5	Esoteric Psychology	16.95
6	Sacred Tarot	15.95
7	Spiritual Astrology	16.95
8	Horary Astrology	11.95
9	Mental Alchemy	11.95
10-1	Natal Astrology: Delineating the Horoscope	12.95
10-2	Natal Astrology: Progressing the Horoscope	14.95
11	Divination and Character Reading	10.95
12-1	Natural Alchemy: Evolution of Life	11.95
12-2	Natural Alchemy: Evolution of Religion	11.95
13	Mundane Astrology	14.95
14	Occultism Applied	16.95
15	Weather Predicting	10.95
16	Stellar Healing	15.95
17	Cosmic Alchemy	14.95
18	Imponderable Forces	10.95
19	Organic Alchemy	11.95
20	The Next Life	15.95
21	Personal Alchemy	14.95
Cards	Egyptian Tarot Card Set (78 Cards)	13.95

Published by
The Church of Light Press, Los Angeles

(see order blank on page 155)

To Order Brotherhood of Light Books:

Qty	Vol #	Item	Price	Amt

Subtotal	
Shipping	
TOTAL	

**Please include shipping & handling charges:
$2.50 first item, $.50 for each additional item.**

☐   **YES ! Please send me a free catalog.**

Ship To:____

Address____

City____

State & Zip Code______________________________________

Telephone____

Send your check or money order to:

**The Church of Light
2341 Coral Street
Los Angeles, CA 90031-2916**